The Maine Event

by Spike Gillespie

Dear Hank,

Thank you for always helping out.

Love, Spike

The Maine Event
Copyright © 2012 by Spike Gillespie

Produced & Published by
March Girls Studio
PO Box 4843
Austin, TX 78765

All rights reserved. No part of this book may be reproduced or transmitted in any form or by any means without written permission from the author.

Some names of people and places have been changed because I don't want to hear folks bitch and moan about my take on things.

Cover design by Erin Mayes of EmDash www.emdashonline.com
Front and back cover photos by Ori Sofer © 2012 & 2011

ISBN (978-0-9883345-1-9)

Printed in USA by 48HrBooks (www.48HrBooks.com)

This one is for Ori Sofer.
Thanks for sticking around and for finally realizing that I am always, always, always right. (Just kidding.)
Love,
Little Hulk

CHAPTER ONE

Way before the fiasco at the Newark Airport nearly obliterated our long-planned Maine vacation, Warren and I had discussed, on numerous occasions and not always pleasantly, cancelling the trip. And though I didn't keep a running tally of these discussions or when they started, knowing us it is entirely possible that within 24 hours of Warren clicking *confirm purchase* for our tickets, I issued my first proclamation to forget it, I wasn't going, he could go without me if he wanted, but I would rather stay home alone and pick full ticks off of the dogs' swollen, unexpressed anal glands than risk an argument-filled week away together.

In truth, threatening to ditch plans (including the relationship itself) is part of our regular dynamic. The stakes simply get higher when we start trip planning. One or the other of us, displeased with some itinerary suggestion, or maybe with something less identifiable like, oh, I don't know, a butterfly taking a shit on the far side of Neptune, will announce *That's it! I'm not going!*

My therapist calls this sort of behavior the Go-Away-Come-Back Game, and points out that it is most often found in two-year-olds testing playground limits with their parents. The child "runs away" to the edge of that squishy faux dinosaur skin stuff demarcating the swing set area. The parent, eventually glancing up from iPhone, vaguely registers that the child is placing itself squarely in the face of potential imminent danger and, irritated at having been interrupted mid-text-message, firmly says "Come back!" The child defies, takes another step away, supposedly not for the pure pleasure of being a pint-sized douche bag, but rather with the secret hope that the parent will react more strongly, come running behind, raise a voice to demonstrate love through dominance, yelling, and control.

Okay, my therapist didn't really include those justifications. I think maybe she concluded with something like, "searching for a sign the parent cares," with the idea that I might connect the dots and see that my threats to leave a relationship are really about my deep-seated desire for a partner to come running behind me, decry my threats to abandon ship, and insist that I *COME BACK RIGHT NOW!!* The implication being, of course, that life just wouldn't be fun without me around.

Though I try to see the possibilities in her theory, I have to say that the first thing that comes to mind when I attempt to dissect the idea is a ridiculous bill of goods my mother used to try to sell me as a child when she insisted that the reason my father regularly yelled at me was because he loved me. Yes, that's right: *Yelling = Love.*

I'm nearly fifty now and have had much time to think about my mother's theory so I feel confident in delivering this verdict: Yelling *because* you love someone is not only oxymoronic in theory, it is pure bullshit in practice. And yet, here I am, decades beyond my childhood, and here Warren is, decades beyond his, and sometimes— hardly unique I'll grant you— we yell at each other. *Because* we love each other? Nah. *In spite of the fact* we love each other? Maybe. *Maybe.* Or maybe the yelling is less anchored in genuine, heat-of-the-moment emotions and instead is far more predictable and rote, rooted almost purely in the respective cultures in which we were raised, and which neither of us has ever fully shaken.

See, Warren is Israeli and I'm from New Jersey and if you ask me— based on a very informal study I did in Tel Aviv, comparing the culture, customs, attitude, and sheer volume (content and decibel) I found there to my experience with those same things growing up in New Jersey— I must say that in some respects Jersey and Israel seem like twins separated at birth. In particular it seems to me that everyone in both places feels a constant need to emphasize everything. And by emphasize I mean *holler*.

So maybe it's as simple as that. Warren and I yell because apparently we can't *not* yell. Yelling is our birthright. If we don't yell, we might die. And yet... and yet I have proclaimed as a goal for years now, even before I met him, that yelling is something I most hope to eliminate from my life.

Am I fooling myself in believing it possible that I can eradicate all or at least most yelling from my life? I think not, though I admit I could be wrong. Maybe yelling and being yelled at is as much my unshakeable fate as these brown eyes and this belly of mine— a paunch just like my grandmother's, my mother's, and those of my seven sisters. Maybe I am just futilely flipping the bird at Fate whenever I proclaim to Warren (often at the top of my lungs) that *WE ARE NOT ALLOWED TO EVER YELL ANYMORE OR ELSE!!!*

Some days I imagine Fate gets a kick out of this little show I put on and, once I've worn myself out hollering, rewards me not with an ovation, but a snarky little refrain: *Here's a hint for ya, hon—if you want to purge yelling from your life, then a) go back in time and don't be born in New Jersey and b) certainly don't have an Israeli for a romantic partner and c) quit fucking yelling already.*

Inability to totally avoid our voluminous destinies notwithstanding, Warren and I have certainly gotten more settled in over our years together. We really do yell less often. And we really have learned how to try to say what we *mean* in the heat of ~~an argument~~ *emphatic discussion* vs. what we know will fuel the fires of melodrama. But back in the early days, *Let's Break Up* was like an anthem for us, pretty much the universal default response to everything, uttered if not weekly then at least biweekly. So, for example:

You really don't like my spanakopita recipe? Fine! Let's break up!

You really think it's okay to stand in front of the open refrigerator and just stare and you aren't worried about wasting energy? That's insane. Let's break up!

You really think it's okay to keep a picture of your stupid, bitchy ex-girlfriend prominently displayed like that—REALLY? That does it! Let's break up!

You really can't sleep without four dogs in the bed? No, seriously, we need to BREAK UP!

Despite our best efforts to change the Let's-Break-Up pattern once we identified it for what it was, everyone knows that old habits die hard, and everyone also knows that anyone who claims to be in a relationship in which there are no arguments: a) has mastered the arts of denial and repression and/or b) is married to an imaginary spouse and or c) is more full of shit than a roomful of constipated Great Danes.

And so, no big surprise, Warren and I are prone to revisit our less savory patterns from time to time. With relapse comes complete dissipation of any progress we've made courtesy of self-help books I've forced Warren to read (*OR ELSE WE ARE BREAKING UP!*). Out the window go exercises in mindfulness relationship conduct. And while these relapses certainly are not limited to trip-planning, that particular activity invariably pushes us over some invisible edge of irritability, perhaps the crankiness born of knowing that much compromise lies ahead of us.

Thus, almost immediately upon booking flights, we become cranky, hungry, sleep-deprived toddlers trapped in middle-aged bodies. And no, not even a keen, anticipatory awareness of our book-a-flight-count-on-a-fight pattern can prevent one or the other of us (most likely both) from uttering at some point: *Oh yeah?*

Really? You want to be like that? Then fine. Why don't you cancel the trip? I don't even want to go with you anyway!

You might think, with this particular affliction, we'd come up with a smarter solution, one that rhymes with Meparate Macations. *Au contraire.* We actually love, love, love traveling together. We've been to Hawaii and Mexico, France and Israel, Canada and all over the states. We've been on road trips and plane trips, ferries and trains. Travel, despite our sometimes grumpy attempts at planning our trips, is one of the things we do best of all together, once we actually get going. Case in point: *The Newark Airport Fiasco of 2011* or, more precisely, our response to it: *Power Twins Unite*!

****

The day starts very early, with me running Warren to the Austin's adorable little airport to catch his ungodly early flight. Because we buy our tickets at discount websites where often you can score, on the cheap, the last remaining seat on a plane, it is not at all unusual for us to wind up on entirely different flights to the same destination on the same day. Such is the case on this day. So I drop him off and zip back to my place, determined to squeeze in one important errand before for my son, Henry, picks me up to take me back to the airport to catch my own flight.

The errand I'm plotting entails a couple of steps, though the goal is simple: deposit a check in the bank so I might have funds for my vacation. Technically this action is not necessary, as Warren and I long ago established a system where he— forever the keeper of a healthful bank account— ponies up the dough for our travel expenses, and later presents me, the less fiscally organized one, with an itemized bill for my share of our spending, which I then pay off in installments.

This spreadsheet-and-invoice routine prompted me to recoil the first time Warren suggested it, when we traveled to Mexico with another couple just a few months into our relationship. There seemed to me to be a coldness to his calculations, his neat mathematics leaving little room for whimsical, impulse buys and the kind of proclamations I have loved to issue my whole life, boisterous sentences that start with, "I'd like to buy…" and conclude with, "a round for the house!!" or "this 1963 Galaxy sedan" or "this full-sized blue plastic throne!"

Warren insisted though, and wrote down all of our expenses and who paid for what. Back home he went over these records, determined who chipped in more than necessary and who owed whom how much to make it all Even Steven. To my surprise I came to greatly appreciate his efforts. I realized that his share-and-share-alike division meant I'd spent far less than I would have had I gone with my usual *Don't-Worry-I-Can-Pay-for-Everybody's-Everything-Every-Time!* big spender routine, when the truth was such splurges left me perpetually wiped out.

That initial lesson, plus several other trips during which we used the Warren-Pays-and-I-Reimburse banking program, drove home the fact that I could rely on him. But still, I liked to know that I could, if I wanted to, access my own mad money on trips. I wanted to be able to— or at least imagine being able to— spend with abandon at fancy restaurants, boutique shops, and high-end patisseries. When we first met, such spending on my part seemed to startle and disturb Warren, a man who thrives on saving money, who buys his uniform articles of clothing— olive cargo shorts and green button-down, short-sleeve shirts— at the thrift store, already well-worn, and then wears them until they have holes in them.

The days of arguing over money are mostly behind us though. Even if I have never come to fully understand his frugality, and even if he sometimes still winces at my kid-in-a-candy-store spending sprees, at least we work to give each other wide berth, agree to disagree. And so I know that on this latest trip Warren will not deny me gleeful souvenir shop jaunts in search of harmonicas shaped like lobster claws, or moose-filled snow globes, or lay even the slightest guilt trip if I decide a stuffed-toy puffin must be acquired.

Yet in my head I am prone to still sometimes assign him the role I'd established before we hammered out our money differences: unbudgeable cheapskate. During these rare occurrences, I reflexively resent Warren, as if he has knotted the purse strings tight and is withholding even times he is not. When these moments arise, I want to disbelieve any generosity he might actually be exhibiting, and cling to the resentful feeling I created, probably in large part so that I can feel a sense of rebellion when I do spend impulsively.

My quick errand to the post office and bank will put a little mad money in my account, momentarily assuage any sense (real or imagined) of feeling beholden to Warren that I might be fostering, and allow me to whip out my own debit card and just pay for things as if I have a small pile of gold in the bank, even if we both know this is a lie, even if I am still paying off my share of last year's trip to Israel, even if the check I'm expecting really should go toward my monthly nut.

Successfully executing Operation Bank Deposit is not without potential obstacles and complications. First, I'm not even sure the check will have yet arrived at the post office where I get my mail. Even if it is, my success will be contingent on my ability to get my hands on my mail. Because it isn't yet 11 am, and the sign in the lobby says all mail will be out by 11 am, which means don't bother asking for your mail if it's before 11 am.

As the holder of a PO Box at this office for sixteen years, I also know not to believe that sign, that they don't always get all the mail out on time. On this particular day, I can't wait, even if they are running on schedule. I have to be at the airport before 10. And so on the drive over, I begin creating and practicing a variety of lines I might use to convince a desk clerk to just see if the anticipated check is lurking in one of the big sorting bins in the back.

Here might be a good time to think about human regard for rules: making them, breaking them, becoming outraged when others break them, becoming more outraged still when we are accused of breaking them, hating the sense of entitlement we sense in others, and feeling more than totally entitled to our own sense of entitlement. Because within moments of crossing the threshold of the post office, I have an opportunity to experience, up close (way too close) and personal (entirely too personal), a full spectrum of rule-related emotions as I unwittingly am drawn to be an active participant in a little improvisational drama I'll call *Talk to the Hand*.

Talk to the Hand

The players:
Spike: Innocent Protagonist.
Tia: Mail clerk known to randomly but regularly puff up and snipe at customers who, increasingly, are being driven to do all of their correspondence via email, since Tia's attitude makes real life postal interactions nearly unbearable.
Supervisor: Short, sallow, sour woman. Clearly hates all humans. Likely would not stop to piss on a man should she find him lying in the gutter with his heart afire.

Scene I

Interior small post office. Daytime. It is a peculiarly slow day, the usual long line for passports is non-existent, and save for one other customer the place is a Ghost Town. Two clerks stand idle. Enter Spike, surprised at the lack of line as she scoots past the faux velvet rope and approaches Tia's station.

Spike: Would you do me a favor? I'm leaving town on vacation and I have to be at the airport before the 11 mail drop. Will you just check to see…

Tia: [Interrupting] GIRL! You *always* going on vacation. I heard you use that line with Phil two weeks ago! I am *NOT* supposed to check the mail early. You gotta wait like everybody else. You *know* the rules! [Tia holds up a hand as if she is auditioning to be a crossing guard.]

Spike: [Internal dialogue] *Fuck this bitch. I don't need a goddamned lecture when a simple no will do. And I sure as hell don't need her to put her hand up to my face.*

Spike: [Aloud] Look I was just asking… I'm waiting on a check…

Tia: [Angrily] *YOU WANT ME TO GET MY SUPERVISOR? That* what you want?

Spike: [At first baffled but then, feeling challenged and taking the bait, feeling irritated.] Uh? Okay? Okay sure! Get your supervisor!

Spike: [Internal dialogue] *Why do these dumbasses have to do this to me? Now I have to get out my Irish Buddhism and teach enlightenment with a virtual nose punch. Crap. I really don't have time for this.*

[Spike waits and waits and fucking waits. Eventually she can see, as she peers through the small space between the curtains dividing front and back, that Tia is headed back out FINALLY, and she is walking with a supervisor. Tia is animatedly telling the supervisor something Spike cannot hear, though she strongly suspects that she— Spike —is being painted as the unreasonable bitch when, in fact, we all know that Tia is the unreasonable bitch!]

Spike: [Internal dialogue]: *Oh great. She's building a case against me, saying I think I'm a princess. This is so unfair. What a total BITCH.*

Supervisor [Emerging from behind curtain with Tia]: What can I do for you?

Spike: I just asked if I could get my mail and she is getting all Talk to the Hand on me and you know what? I DON'T NEED ANYONE GOING ALL TALK TO THE HAND ON ME.

Supervisor: [Flatly, as if recently prescribed Paxil has just kicked in.] We can't just be getting your mail for you early.

Spike: Let me tell you something…

Supervisor: [Interrupting]: It's in big bins back there and…

Spike: [Defensive] LOOK I JUST *ASKED* OKAY. SHE COULD JUST SAY NO. BUT NO, SHE'S ALL *TALK TO THE HAND!!!*

*[In a moment of utter absurdity, Tia puts two envelopes down on the counter. Despite the big hullabaloo, she **has** gotten the mail, even though it's "breaking the rules" and even though the supervisor is saying it can't be done. Spike notes that one envelope is, in fact, the anticipated check. This should be enough to quiet her. She should take the money and run. But, no. Too late. Button pushed. Must engage! Must engage!]*

Supervisor: *Shhh…*

Spike: DON'T SHUSH ME!

Supervisor: I am trying to run a business here.

Spike: Yeah well guess what? As recently as *YESTERDAY* my mail was put out *AFTER 11!!!* So if you guys are going to break the rules and *NOT PUT MY MAIL OUT ON TIME* then *I CAN BREAK THE RULES AND ASK FOR IT EARLY!* Tia? Tia, I want to say something to you!

Tia: [Averting eyes] Unh-*uh!* I am not talking to you! You talk to *HER!* [Gestures to supervisor.]

Spike: But I want to talk to *YOU!* I have to see *YOU* every day. I want to RESOLVE THIS!

Tia: Unh-*uh!* No. [Again makes Talk to the Hand gesture.]

Supervisor: [Feeling attacked] Our mail is *not* put out late.

Spike: [Foolishly and indignantly, refusing to just take the money and run, stands her ground because sometimes playing the role of an idiot is entirely too tempting to resist.] YES IT IS!

Supervisor: I'm going to have to investigate this.

[Exit Spike, hissing JESUS CHRIST as she storms out, though at least she has the check and really, WAS THAT SO FUCKING HARD TO DO ON A LINE-FREE DAY IN AN EMPTY POST OFFICE FOR A CUSTOMER WHO HAS PAID $1000 OVER THE YEARS TO A FAILING INSTITUTION FOR THE 'PRIVILEGE' OF HAVING HER MAIL PUT OUT LATE HALF THE TIME? REALLY?!!!]

Driving away from the post office, I am angry. I am angry for many reasons. First and foremost I am angry because I am angry, because I keep trying to rid myself of anger and Be A Better Person Than That. I'm also angry because why does Tia have to be such a fucking bitch? And if I'm really honest, I guess I'm angry because I asked for special privileges—which Phil the nice clerk often extends me— and I got rebuffed and chastised.

Rebuffed and *chastised.* These are two of my three biggest big buttons (being mocked the third). Shot down. Told no. Treated like I'm "bad." I know, I know— we're all weary of contemplating the psych underpinnings of why certain things prompt us, without fail, to go bananas. But indulge me please and allow me to acknowledge that, yes, I think that the fact my father rebuffed and chastised me my entire miserable childhood is, with all certainty, the reason I want to instantly punch out (well, okay— more like yell at) anyone whose behavior prompts in me an emotional flashback to those days.

Beyond the violent urge lies something worse still. Because even though I know I can and will refrain from literal fisticuffs, I know just as certainly that I won't be able to easily shake this episode. Which means that I am going to be taking Tia with me on vacation. She has suddenly become my unwanted extra baggage and there will be a high price to pay for bringing her along. Also, there's no way she's going to fit in the overhead compartment or under the seat in front of me. Oh no, Tia is going to be riding inside my head, taking up way more mental real estate than I can actually afford to offer her. She has set the tone. I have let her set the tone.

Crap.

CHAPTER TWO

It is in this frame of mind that I scoot from the post office over to my credit union, a few blocks away, to deposit the check. The poison of my anger at Tia is already taking effect as I wonder how the bank clerk might piss me off. Anticipated aggravation does not occur, but that's beside the point. I have shifted from my normal state of *Extremely Sensitive with Somewhat Manageable Chip on Shoulder* to *On The Lookout for a Fight with Boulder on Shoulder*, and sadly, my awareness is not enough to help me slough off this defensive armor. I'm just going to have to wait out this foul mood.

Henry is not quite awake when I pull into his driveway, and he stumbles out into the Texas sunshine like a naked mole rat emerging from underground for the very first time, blinking uselessly against the blinding light. His massive mess of hair all over the place, eye boogies still punctuating his tear ducts, skinny black jeans tattooed to his endlessly long skeleton legs.

"Mornin'" he says in an octave so deep it still startles me, like some unknown-to-me incident when he was 14 found him victim of *Invasion of Leonard Cohen and the Voice Snatchers*. That one word is about all he has to offer for the short drive to the airport, his laconic state a cross between the early (for him) hour and, let's face it, the fact that twenty-year-old males don't typically have that much to share with their middle-aged mothers.

In my haste to get to the airport, as well as my growing consumption with my un-put-downable irritation with Tia, I totally forget to perform the one ritual that has marked so many of my departures from the time Henry was three. That year, as I readied to go on an extremely rare trip without him, I sat him down for a talk. Before I tell you what I said, and before you judge me for this, please bear in mind that I was a single mother and so I had an overblown but not entirely irrational concern about my son's well-being should I die while he was little and leave him alone in the world. Plus, from the moment he was born I was determined to correct (okay *over-correct*) all of my parents' child-rearing errors, which certainly included a perpetual lack of information.

And so, wanting to prepare my young son for all possibilities, I had a chat with him that had seemed perfectly reasonable to me when I was mentally formulating it, and only revealed itself as stupid as it left my mouth and reached my ears. "Honey," I said, looking into his big, brown eyes, holding his chunky little toddler hand. "I want you to know that if mommy's plane crashes, you have got to carry on. Don't be sad. Just have fun. It's like the *Lion King*— the circle of life. I'll always be right there, up in the sky." (Dramatically points to sky.)

For those of you who are contemplating but have not yet tried over-honesty with your small child, let me be over-honest here. The look of sheer horror that crossed little Henry's face when I suggested my plane might crash suggested that, the best laid plans of mice and men and all that, perhaps I had overdone my efforts to cover all bases. To his credit, he was able to eventually turn this never-to-be-forgotten conversation into a lifelong joke, or at least pretend to tolerate it when, as the years passed and he grew older and I began to take more solo trips, I would precede each departure with, "Honey, if anything happens to me, you know what to do?"

Dutifully, he would respond, "Carry on, your wayward son…"

"That's right!"

It was only when he was nineteen that my amusing child decided to exact gentle revenge. Heading to play a gig in Mexico— where the cartels were fond of kidnapping, murdering, beheading and dismembering random victims on a daily basis— he said, in his most understated tone, "Hey mom— if anything happens to me, *carry on.*"

Point taken. The game didn't end entirely on that note but, as on this day, we now had times where it remained blessedly forgotten. The drop-off then proceeds without unnecessary drama. "Have a good trip," he says, very deeply, before chugging off in my little car.

In the terminal, I get confirmation that Tia has indeed come along for the ride. This despite me trying to convince her to just stay in Austin and enjoy her time without me. I cannot get right with her, or with my own head. I continue to seesaw, angry at how she treated me, angry at myself for taking the bait, for responding to her hissy fit with my own, and all the while wondering when I will forget her. Is it sad that this is how I define "amazing growth"— that I can at least recognize that I am angry and know, if only vaguely, that the anger will pass even though it feels like it won't?

On the plane, cramped into my tiny allotted space, it dawns on me that I am apparently sitting directly behind the man, the myth, the legend— Mr. Paul Bunyan— and that PB, though we haven't even taken off yet, is pressing back as hard as he can on his already reclined seat in a semi-successful attempt to spend the flight resting in my lap like a very large Pekinese. I figure it'll take five minutes or less for a set of colicky triplets and their frayed parents to cram into the seats behind me. I exhale. I try to get into vacation head. Despite the ridiculous conditions of flying these days— the cost of the ticket, the cost to check a suitcase, the cost of headphones, of snacks, of thinking impure thoughts, of taking a crap that lasts longer than five minutes, of looking out the window without permission from the pilot, of sneezing— I love flying. I love it. I love it because for one, I am no longer terrified of it as I was for years. That is more than a little progress.

I also love it because flying means I am going away. And I love it because it means that no one can contact me via phone, email or knock on the door for however many hours I am in the air. (Yes, in-flight wifi is becoming a thing. No, I have not had access to it yet and I think I'd like to keep it that way.) I have finally broken my habit of buying PEOPLE magazine before boarding— sue me but honestly Angelina just doesn't do it for me plus who the fuck are all these so-called reality "stars"? I no longer have any idea who any of these people are.

Instead, I find my reading material in the form of the menu, tucked away in the back of the in-flight magazine. I peruse the short list of selections with a cross between gravity and giddiness, like an Ultra-Orthodox rabbi studying the Talmud. Discovering that the Middle Eastern Delight Snax Box weighs in at under ten bucks, I decide what the heck, I'm on vacation, *I'm getting the fucking Middle Eastern Delight Snax Box!*

The flight attendants, as they are wont to do, are sashaying about the cabin in that old divide-and-conquer routine: one with the food cart, the other with the beverage cart, the pair of them sporting matching don't-fuck-with-me expressions. I wait for the food-half of the duo to lean in and take my order. Instead, she rolls right on by.

I feel the dragon of my persecution complex snort a little fire into my brain. I quiet the dragon and say, *We mustn't take this personally*. I tell myself that surely there has been a mistake and that she will be back. I remind myself that the ghost of Tia is haunting me, and this paranoia is all her fault. Despite these tactics and though I am not even actually hungry, the thought that now I might not get my fucking Middle Eastern Delight Snax Box sends my inner Hunter Gatherer on high alert.

Must. Get. Fucking. Snax. Box.

My tendency toward perseveration kicks in and I begin to concoct conspiracy theories in which the neglectful flight attendant has singled me out for purposeful neglect. But before I can establish a full laundry list of possibilities, another flight attendant, he of the beverage cart, speaks to me, interrupting my complex case-building process.

"What would you like to drink?" he asks. He has a honking Jersey accent, the kind of accent I grew up with, and ran away from, and got rid of in my own voice. The kind of accent that now— probably because I'm turning into a sappy middle ager— I sort of like hearing, my ears perking up at the sound of it, a response that reminds me, in a way, of how my dogs just cannot resist sniffing the shit of other dogs.

"What about a Snax Box?" I say.

"But she just came by with the food cart, I'm in charge of drinks," he says. Straightforward enough, save for the fact that I've got the Tia filter on and so what my ears hear sounds more like, *"You had your chance, bitch. You let her pass. Don't lie to me and try to tell me that she didn't offer you food. I know she did. You're one of those passengers that likes to make it hard on us, aren't you? Do you need me to call an air marshal? Talk to the hand!"*

"She didn't offer me a Snax Box!" I protest.

Flight Attendant Two disappears then, allowing me time to really go over in my head, in minute detail, just how fucking rude he just was to me. Did he actually imply that I had *planned* a scheme where I would *ignore* the First Flight Attendant just so I could turn the tables and suggest she ignored me, all so I can get her in trouble? *REALLY?* How *DARE* he!! What a *cocksucker!*

And then, before I can add to that list some other choice descriptions, I am startled again out of my stupor by this very same man who has quietly reappeared and is saying, "Here ya go, hon!"

21

Then, cheerful as can be, he hands me the goods with what passes for a smile. My Fucking Snax Box! My Coke Zero! My little cup of perfect little airplane ice cubes! It looks right but something is confusing here. Wait. Rewind. Did he, this man who five minutes ago snapped at me, just call me *hon*? And did he call me *hon* in a honking Jersey accent? And was it tinged with what passes for genuine sweetness in Jersey?

He did and it was. And with that little verbal gesture, that gentle caress of my ears with his voice, I feel a near instant and utterly palpable shift in my attitude. I feel a release. I feel like things are going to be okay. Because I realize now that his first part of the spiel—that brusque *blattety blah blah* about how I should've ordered when I had the chance— was just a moment of Pure Jersey. No harm meant. One minute you get snapped at. The next minute you're *hon*. This is just how it works in my homeland.

Mulling this internal shift— how just the minute before I longed to rip off his head and shit down his lungs, and how now I want to nuzzle his earlobes and let him scratch between my ears— I think: *Is it any wonder that I have spent my entire life on guard?* And, more importantly, can I please hang onto this moment of Zen and remember that things are not always what they seem or that at least they will shift and shift again?

CHAPTER THREE

Though I left Austin a couple of hours after him, Warren's kooky layover configuration has him landing in Jersey later than me. Anyone who doesn't own a private jet but who does travel by plane will have no trouble recognizing that this is not at all unusual in the current, ever-disintegrating world of commercial air transportation, aka The Best Way to Annoy a Large Number of People in a Fairly Short Amount of Time.

My own flight is delayed thanks to bad weather that dictates we circle the runway for an hour before landing. Even with this lag though, I manage to get there first and, without the Frugal Hand of Warren to deter me, I pop into a fancy (for an airport) deli, select a couple of wildly overpriced (natch) sandwiches— turkey and brie for him, fresh mozzarella with basil and tomato for me— to wolf down once I do locate him.

This tracking process, normally a snap courtesy of cell phones, is hindered since Warren forgot his phone at home. At least he realized this oversight before taking off from Austin, and so used a borrowed phone to leave me a message, which I fortunately received in time to double back to his place and grab it. A nice gesture but, for the moment, not helpful—calling him will simply ring the phone in my backpack.

Whatever concern I have about not being able to call Warren is assuaged momentarily by the memory of White Courtesy Phone days when you could actually, rather easily, page someone in an airport. And while the airline rep I approach to inquire if this practice is still possible refuses to page Warren, he does seem happy enough to look up Warren's flight information for me, without asking me to produce any sort of identification to prove that I am actually connected to the person for whom I am soliciting private data.

Being able to readily access from an airline rep that to which I have no legal right gives me the same little excited buzz I get whenever I manage to clear security without pulling out my toiletry bag or being caught smuggling in a 5 oz. tube of toothpaste (practicing in my head the line: *"Oh I am so sorry! Dear me! I plum forgot!"* just in case I get busted by TSA).

Hard to pinpoint the perverse pleasure I take in airline agents not following protocol or forcing me to jump through dozens of flaming post-911 security hoops, but maybe my satisfaction derives from the notion that we're all human, prone to mistakes. Or that I can, if only rarely, still weasel information out of people the way I could in the old days, if I ask just right.

And— if I am to be totally honest— I also love knowing that, thanks to one of these blatant gaffes, if I find myself in a pinch later on, I can raise holy hell if I feel I have been mistreated ("being mistreated" being pretty much synonymous with "flying coach") by pointing out that so-and-so skirted protocol. (I hear myself, in my imagination, on the phone with customer service, seeking six-figure compensation for lost baggage and the accompanying pain and suffering of having to go without clean underwear on vacation, and then, upon being told "compensation for lost baggage is not policy," I reply: *"NOT **POLICY**? REALLY? **NOT POLICY**? YOU WANT TO TALK ABOUT **NOT POLICY**? HOW ABOUT THIS? YOUR AGENT GAVE ME PRIVATE FLIGHT INFO FOR MY BOYFRIEND WITHOUT ASKING FOR MY IDENTIFICATION! WHAT KIND OF A SHODDY SHIP ARE YOU PEOPLE RUNNING OVER THERE ANYWAY?!!! OR ARE YOU GOING TO TELL ME IT'S POLICY TO HAND*

OUT PRIVATE PASSENGER INFORMATION TO ANY SCHMUCK WHO ASKS FOR IT?!!!")

Imagining a future angry conversation with an airline representative causes two effects. The first, a one-two punch, starts with a montage, an avalanche of mental images of countless outbursts I've had over the years— many in airports, more than a few at retail stores— with workers who *won't give me what I want.* This parade of memories is accompanied by wild emotional seesawing between self-mortification and self-righteousness, where I argue with myself vehemently about how wrong those encounters were but wait *no they weren't because some of those jerks deserved to be yelled at.*

The second effect, riding hard on the heels of the first, is a flashback to the Talk to the Hand Incident with Tia at the post office just that morning. Jesus H. I don't care if Tia was wrong. I just want her out of my head. Out, out, damn Tia! But no, she's stuck there. And I know why she's stuck there. She's stuck there because I really, truly do want to no longer be the person who mixes it up angrily with cashiers and airline employees even in the rare instances where there is a very clear right and a very clear wrong and I very clearly am the former. Because over the years and through these confrontations, I have won lots of battles but lost countless wars in the process.

I like to think (hope) that jerky behavior— even if I do have "just cause"— is almost entirely a thing of my past now. Yes, I have the skills to morph into an enraged and flaming asshole in the blink of an eye. Yes, I have employed these skills on many more occasions than I care to remember or admit. But experience suggests that karma is real and the residual mortification that continues to haunt me even now over some long past incidents has finally gotten me to contemplate, and eventually even sometimes implement, the gorgeous act of walking away.

This Walk Away Wisdom is something my long-ago Taekwondo instructors tried to impart, a concept that did not fully compute for me until years after I left the dojo: Just because you have developed the skills to kill someone with your bare hands and feet is no reason to actually trot out this talent. *Ever.* Far better and far more disciplined is the act of removing oneself from the situation. *Every time.* Initially this made no sense to me. Why train for hundreds of hours over several years to, in essence, not ever do the very thing for which you had trained?

Eventually though, I came to like the idea. As with any concept I come around to adopting, once I decided walking away was a viable and even desirable option, the *idea* of mastering it became dizzyingly exciting even if early *actual results* (read: UTTER FAILURE) yielded frequent bouts of self-flagellation. Very similar to any fledgling self-improvement efforts really. One vows: "I will not eat the chocolate cake/smoke the delicious cigarette/drink the icy cold gin and tonic/scream at the stupid clerk today and I will feel better for this action in the form of inaction!!" And one often follows up, not long after, by devouring the cake/sucking on the cancer stick/slurping down the boozy beverage/getting up in the grille of the innocent cashier. This failure then followed by some internal dialogue that, boiled down, always translates to: "I suck."

But Taekwondo is all about practice and now that I think about it, it's not a huge surprise that as I was winding down my TKD practice, I was also coming to accept a truth about myself I did not like: I am an alcoholic. Let me be clear— one of the biggest things I did not like about admitting this was that admitting it meant also admitting I had to stop. Which I didn't want to do because there was an awful lot about drinking that I loved, or thought I loved, stuff that just so happened to be outweighed (exponentially as I would come to realize) by the bad shit.

But I did quit drinking, and I did sometimes still practice my kicks, and with the hard-won self-discipline of sobriety and martial art forms, I did at least take tiny steps toward the art of putting things down, letting things go, walking away before my temper got out of hand. But still, some days— as on this day— the walking away only happened after I executed, with my sharp tongue, the equivalent of using a double back jump kick to snap a toothpick in half.

Overkill. That was at the root of the Tia-haunting I was suffering. I'd taken a long, tall drink of poison when I tangled with her. I had not walked away, and my anger hangover had been immediate and continued even now, hovering at a sustained, head-splitting pitch, ultimately leaving me far more irritated with myself than with her.

There is a silver lining to both literal and metaphorical hangovers though— hangovers being what prompted me to finally quit drinking, my desire to not feel sick a powerful motivator. My emotional hangover from Tia annoys me enough that I know with certainty I won't ever use this airline clerk's kindness as a weapon in a later angry phone call to customer service. I just feel pure gratitude for his help, his willingness to bend the rules to help me figure out at which gate Warren will be arriving.

Happily, our cost-saving flight plan does not have us merely crossing paths in Newark for a quick, shared dinner of overpriced sandwiches. We have scored seats for the same flight for the final leg of our journey, a little hop from Newark to the Portland Jetport (they actually call it that, a Jetport, as if it is a hub for commuters flying over in jetpacks). I take no small measure of comfort knowing we'll be flying together. Despite the reality that our method of acquiring budget tickets will leave us seated in different sections of the plane, I can still whip up a little you-and-me-against-the-world narrative, at least until we board, me humming that

Sinead O'Connor line I so love about how, *"You used to hold my hand when the plane took off..."*

After finding each other at what was supposed to have been our departure gate, Warren and I are then advised of a gate change. At the new gate, we settle in to gnaw on our sandwiches, and listen as a man announces, with genuine regret (possibly because he understands the imminent fallout for himself and his fellow airline employees): "Folks, I'm sorry I have to make this announcement at all, but *all flights* have been *cancelled*. Please proceed to the nearest service desk to rebook your flights."

Did he really say *all* flights? That can't be right. Because nearby, just a little while later, a huge group cheer goes up— a cheer worthy of the news that cancer has been cured, or Dick Cheney has died, or Waldo has been located— that seems connected to some muffled announcement about another plane that will be taking off for Phoenix after all. Maybe this is it— east and northbound flights: shit out of luck. You on the westward ho routes, not to worry.

Since our last leg was to have gone both east and north, Warren and I are screwed. The old me would've started bitching immediately upon realizing this. The new me—the *I-have-been-meditating-for-twelve-years-now* me, the *I-am-still-feeling-shitty-about-getting-pissed-at-the-Post-Office* me — tells myself to suck it up. The new me, has not yet discovered today's Threshold of Impatience, which, it turns out— spoiler alert—will be located precisely 147 minutes from the all-flights-cancelled message.

But we're not there yet. For the moment, I am the picture of calm, telling myself this will be resolved, it must be resolved, that surely sometime before the end of the year, and probably much, much sooner than that, this situation will have played itself out, and I will be in a place where I can look back, and laugh, and tell the funny story of *that time in the airport when everyone's flights got cancelled, hahahahahaha*!

Initially, this wave of giddiness I feel mutates into a hint of smugness regarding my self-perceived enlightenment, my philosophically superior attitude about my cancelled flight. *No biggie. We'll get there eventually. I really pity all these people complaining so much. Aren't they just happy to be alive?* I stand patiently, laughingly even, in the long line to which we whose flights have just have been cancelled— approximately 750,000 people best as I can tell— have been sent to straighten things out.

I listen to the whiny, overly tanned senior citizens in front of us, and concur with Warren that one of them does look like he could be Steve Buscemi's father. These snowbirds, Yankees that have transplanted themselves from Long Island to Miami for retirement, with their grating nasal accents and leathery skin, call to mind some ill-conceived confection, like poop-covered, unsweetened lemon drops. And lo, the couple behind us, poor old souls, are *going to miss their flight to Rome!!!* This in turn means they are going to *miss their cruise around Greece!!!*

I figure it will probably only cause a fight if I spin around and said, *Yo, bitches, listen up—six million Jews died in the Holocaust. So shut your pieholes about Greece, eh?* Instead I try to cultivate a little compassion for them, try to summon up some of the philosophy gleaned from the memoir I'm currently reading, *Healing: A Woman's Journey from Doctor to Nun*, by Sister Dang Nghiem, a Vietnamese refugee who trained for a career in medicine before answering the call to become a Buddhist nun. *We all have pain. We mustn't judge others.*

Or, if we must judge, better to spread the judgment around a little bit. Cutting the wrinkly brown cruise ship clients a momentary break, I allow my gaze to fall and then linger upon a couple of very young women behind me— if they are over 18, then just barely.

With heavy denim, ankle-length skirts and long, straight hair spilling out from old-school babushkas, they call far more attention to themselves than if they'd been revealing thong-enhanced ass cracks and major cleavage courtesy of pube-grazing low riders and tiny super-scoop tees stretched over Victoria's Secret pushup bras.

Even back when I hated flying I always loved airports for this reason: the pure concentration of human specimens from all walks provides a constant, sustained visual orgasm for people-watching zealots like me. Unless I am doubled over with jet lag, I can sit contentedly for hours on end in airport terminals just taking in the Big Freak Show. (Warren had been so dismayed when he first heard our trip to Israel included an eight-hour layover at Charles De Gaulle in Paris. Not me—I nearly wet my *pantalones* with joy at the prospect of so much time to just drink in all the fashion statements, all the fashion crimes.) I love making up stories about airport people and these young women in their Little House on the Prairie in the Terminal getups offer fodder aplenty.

At first I simply eavesdrop as I try to establish which cult they might belong to. Then I flat out ask, "Uh, do you mind if I ask you…"

You know, in hindsight, I can't remember what in the hell I asked them exactly. In hindsight I'm sort of surprised I asked them at all. What is it about airports that makes everyone all nosy and overly conversational, the whole lot of us suffering from CSC (*Collective Situational Chutzpah*)? Don't answer that. I already know. It's the whole transitional nature of the place. You're not going to see the other person ever again, so why not be a nosy fucker, why not pry for information and push unsolicited advice and wrinkle your nose and interrogate away?

So ask I do. The young lasses explain they've just been to Europe on a pilgrimage. Talking to them a bit about their beliefs reminds me of a time in my life when I dated a very heavy man. I remember thinking, too often, how open-minded I was for not judging him for being so overweight. I took silent pride in my generosity and non-judgment. Until, of course, I realized that if you're walking around thinking about how much you're not thinking about how fat someone is, then you are, in fact, thinking just that.

Likewise these chicks in their American Girl getups. I pretend to be all *different-strokes-for-different-strokes* in my mind, but I don't need to scratch very deeply, or even at all, to see the neon sign flashing my true feelings, which go approximately like this: HOW THE FUCK DO PEOPLE CONTINUE TO GET ROPED INTO THESE STUPID MOTHERFUCKING CULTS?

From there, I can't help but create narratives in which one will just get in deeper and deeper and bear the cult leader fifteen anemic, premature babies, while the other one will have an equal and opposite reaction, and, driven by desires of capitalism and flesh, will flee this Holy Roller scene inside of two years, start dressing like a whore and take up with some big hairy Harley dude (or, better yet, dudette), eventually scoring a book deal or reality show to reveal the cult leader for who he really is.

The pilgrims don't strike me as especially forthcoming, their self-righteousness boiling just beneath the surface. But perhaps they need me for their cause, just as I need them for purposes of entertainment and yet another reminder that I am never going to get the hang of this non-judgment stuff I keep reading about in my Buddhist books. Maybe they know that my faux cheerful tone is but a thin veil. Maybe they are, as I'm speaking, translating this to a sort of persecution, and what's a good and pious Christian pilgrim without a little persecution to prompt the turning of the other cheek? In this sense, then, we are lucky to have found each other!

Maybe this is what I love best about airports. In this concentration of humanity— whiny, over-tanned seniors bemoaning missed cruise ships; adolescent Jesus freaks in LOOK AT ME modest-wear; detached and pushy businessmen, wearing out their opposable thumb joints on Blackberries; sleepy crying children who would rather be home— I have my pick of the litter of *Topics for Internal Dialogues on the Importance of Self-Improvement.*

I first became truly conscious of this possibility for other (extremely annoying) human beings to spur awakening when I attended a Buddhist retreat with Thich Nhat Hanh in 2007. The knowledge was handed to me by a tiny, ancient Buddhist nun who, upon learning from her teenage interpreter, also a nun, that I had just nearly come to blows with another attendee, responded by bursting out laughing.

In a lifetime of interesting experiences, being laughed at by a teeny-tiny 80-year-old Vietnamese woman with a shaved head, in front of a group of people who have solemnly gathered to process deep grief, stands out as a truly unique and unforgettable moment. I had signed up for the retreat in large part to deal with the borderline insanity my most recent divorce had unleashed in me. Others in our afternoon "family circle" included members who had lost a child (or two) or been through other momentous tragedies, experiences that made my legal departure from a ten-month marriage to a raging narcissist embarrassingly negligible in the Life's Hard Knocks category.

And here I came one day, huffing and puffing into our daily group session, enraged that, only moments before, some asshole had shushed me as I tried to console a faraway friend on the phone. Phones were not forbidden at Buddhist camp. Frowned on? Maybe. Verboten? *Nein.* And so I had tripped off down a trail, to make this call out of earshot, mindful of not disturbing the others. A fellow attendee happened to hike by me while I was deep in conversation. When he got about fifty yards past me, he turned and shouted something down at me. What *was* he saying? I wondered.

And then I figured it out. He was yelling sarcastic remarks at me.

"Can't I use this mountain, too?!!" he bellowed, by which he meant, *Pardon me, I'm a loud, domineering dick disguised as a peace loving Buddhist and I am using angry sarcasm to shame you and I am yelling to let you know you are talking too loud!*

There are few things in this world than chap my ass more than being shushed, particularly by a man. To say I dislike being silenced is an understatement akin to saying Stevie Nicks just, you know, sort of liked her cocaine.

So I went after him.

"Excuse me," I said, when I found him on the edge of a cliff. "Are you the guy who just YELLED at me?"

"That's your perception," he hissed, launching into a sort of Zen Orwellian doublespeak that gives Westerners who claim Buddhism as their path a very bad name.

"Do you want to know what I was doing?" I asked. "I was counseling a friend in crisis!!"

"And now you're confronting me!" he said, and he shushed me again.

Oh, Buddha help me. That did it. I busted out my most angry line, given the fact a huge statue of Buddha was watching over us. "You are making me *very* unhappy," I said.

"You unhappiness is an obstacle of your own creation," he replied, smugly.

I walked away. He came after me. "So you're just going to walk away?"

"You never would have yelled at me if I were a man,"

"Not true," he said. "That's just your issue to work on."

"No, my work is to rip off your head and shit down your lungs, asshole," I said. Okay, so I didn't really say that. But I wanted to.

This is the story I related, with some language modifications, when I arrived breathless at my meditation circle. After the young translator spelled it out for the very old nun, she began to laugh and laugh. She said something in Vietnamese. Her interpreter now began to laugh.

"She said to tell you he is your bell," giggled the teenage nun. "Whenever you encounter someone like this, it's your gift. A reminder to be mindful."

My gift? Really?

The rest of the group laughed. Okay, I laughed, too. And I discovered, as the years marched on, that sometimes these pithy pronouncements really do hold a lot of weight. Surely this is why when I am, say, confronting barely post-pubescent airport pilgrims, a little bell is going off in my head reminding me to take a closer look at what about these different-than-me people is getting my Judgment Knickers in a massive twist. How I hate to admit that sometimes (okay, *often*) what's getting to me is some part of my own self I'm not crazy about being reflected back. I might not be sporting a head hanky or holding tickets to a Greek Cruise, but scrutiny, that bitch, is often bound to reveal our annoying similarities to those who most annoy us, if we just give her the chance.

CHAPTER FOUR

When an airline rep approaches our line, which resembles an extremely long, extremely lethargic anaconda, to announce there's another line "over there," Warren and I, like all of the others comprising this joyless, stagnant assembly, need to make a decision whether to conga on over to another counter or continue to take our chances here. Even under the best, calmest, most pressure-free circumstances, we— individually and as a couple— often find ourselves stumped in the face of decision-making. This is yet another factor that differentiates us from the young, denim-skirted, head-covered Jesus freaks who, quicker than you can say *Beelzebub*, have already made a beeline for this other line, disappearing so swiftly as to suggest the Rapture has just occurred.

Warren and I— perpetual wafflers or deeply thoughtful pragmatists depending on how you look at it— consider how, by the time we get to this other "over there" line, we might well find ourselves in an even larger herd of people who took the gamble, convinced themselves the new line would be shorter and lost. We also consider how the line we're in hasn't moved an inch in forty minutes. This is when Warren starts wondering out loud if maybe we should "just go back to Austin."

To my credit, I recognize such ponderings as button pushers. Not on par with being told to shush or that I'm wrong, but still with the sort of irritant effect that will, I guarantee, not produce anything even close to a pearl. I tell myself I am not going to take the bait. I am going to breathe through this. This little hitch in the giddy-up of our travel plans is hardly the end of the world.

In fact, it is nowhere in the vicinity of the end of the world. This is, without question, a First World Problem. Because while we might be starting to feel stressed out, the big picture reality is that we are just fine. To wit:

We are indoors.

Our bellies are full.

We are not forced by our beliefs to wear floor-length denim and headscarves.

We have experienced a wonderful surprise blessing: The "We'll miss our cruise!" whiners have gone the way of the pilgrims, giving us a break from their incessant bemoaning of situation.

So there's all that. Plus, I know that we'll know, within twenty-four hours, what we decided. That might sound stupid or weird or obvious or not at all obvious. But reminding myself that soon enough I'll be able to look back and see how it all went down sometimes helps to keep me in the moment, *in the moment* being the number one most difficult place to locate at any given moment even if, duh, the given moment is both the only moment you have and the one which you seek. I remind myself to not spiral back and dwell on, say, the time in the San Francisco airport when Henry was little and our flight was delayed due to airline stupidity and I made a scene and a desk monkey pretended he wanted to be helpful but actually picked up the phone and pretended to call security to try to frighten me into submission (he won that round).

I also remind myself not to catapult into some unknown future and create a narrative in which, say, after years of telling Warren he just *has* to come with me to Maine, we got SO CLOSE but we MISSED IT and THE WORLD SUCKS. I just say— at least until my patience wears thin two hours and twenty-seven minutes into this ordeal— that I am okay right here, right now, not the victim of Mexican drug cartels or Somali pirates. Just a white, middle-aged, middle-class, healthy woman, living in a free country, mildly inconvenienced by an unexpected extended layover in Jersey which, even though this is the place my traumatic childhood took place, that's all behind me now and, hey, look at that! *Something else to be grateful for!!*

This is how, at least for fifteen seconds, I avoid getting annoyed or exasperated with Warren's sudden doomsayer stance, his questioning the wisdom and feasibility of trying to get from Newark to Maine in a timely fashion. But it's hard to block out his pessimism, which seems to be taking on the characteristics of one of those little vacuum-packed sponges that looks all flat and innocent until you pop it in a little water and, *voila*, it springs into something much bigger. I don't want to acknowledge the bigger truth, but we both know the truth lurks, threatens to foil. That truth is this: While the cranky, orangey-tan senior citizens are running the risk missing a cruise, Warren and I are also in danger of missing the boat, the ferry that runs from Port Clyde, Maine out to Monhegan Island.

The boat only runs three times per day, and to get to it you have to drive two hours from the Portland Jetport. This two-hour drive comes *after* however the hell long it takes to rent a car and provided there is no major traffic backup along the tiny one-lane roads from point A to point B. And there are other factors to consider:

Ferry captains aren't keen on waiting for late tourists, in fact it might just be possible they get a kick out of watching latecomers race to the dock two minutes too late.

The place we are scheduled to stay on the island, The Monhegan House, is only open for two more days. Saturday night is the last night of the season.

So even if we do have the time and money and patience to wait for another flight, any delay means we'll be shit out of luck in the accommodations department. Either we get to Maine by the last ferry of the next day or we might as well not go at all. That seems to be the bigger point Warren is making, though my ears are having a hard time not hearing, *"You know, I really don't care if I never see Maine, so what say we just cut our losses and head back home now?"*

I inform Warren that we are going to Maine. I want to get to Maine. I will not *not* go to Maine. Some of this attitude is just the obstinacy with which I was born. But much of it is rooted in knowledge I have and Warren lacks: Maine is crazy fucking gorgeous, full of curious and laconic folk who— at least as best as I can tell— genuinely do not give a shit what the rest of the world thinks. The scenery ranges from quaint to rugged, historic and cozy to wild and breathtaking. Houses hundreds of years old, mammoth moose, flaming autumn leaves, twisty little roads, ancient cemeteries. The first time I vacationed here— the place isn't called Vacationland for nothing— I knew I had to come back and that I had to come back often. I don't care if we have to hitchhike. We *are* going to Maine.

Okay, okay then— let's go check out the other line. This is the decision we come to after much debate. What is the name of this phenomenon where even when you know that choosing Action A is going to bring Equal and Opposite and Negative Reaction B, you can't stop yourself from taking that first action? For example, I have a horrible sense of direction. One of my co-feminists tells me this is just learned helplessness, ingrained from a childhood of being told that girls can't do certain things. I assure you that my dear friend's theory is pure and utter bullshit. I am simply so directionally challenged that I could make a case for a new syndrome, SRD— Spatial Relations Dyslexia.

For example, let's say I am trying to get somewhere and I think, "Now which way should I turn?" No matter which way I ultimately do turn, it is *always* the wrong way. This is true even if I attempt a preemptive strike of damage control by saying, "Okay, you know you always go the wrong way, so your brain is saying go left, if you go right then you can't go wrong." So then I go right and it's *still* wrong. Like my brain is outsmarting itself in stupidity.

Along these lines, Warren and I are pretty confident that if we do go to the other line it will be longer. But if we don't go it will be shorter. Instead of staying put, and even knowing that something about our mere presence in the other line will slow it down, we can't resist going. And once again we prove the effects of this unnamed law, which, from now on, I will refer to the Wrong Airport Line Law (WALL). Not only that, but we are now back in line with the Missed-Cruise-Ship Complaint Department, headed up by Steve Buscemi, Sr., and the Maxi Denim Skirts for God Patrol, co-captained by the young brides of Jesus.

As sure as bears shit in the woods and popes wear funny hats and Al Gore was robbed, this other line is long. Very. At least as long as the one we just got out of. Not only long, but moving at about the pace of a recently salted slug. I extract my knitting from the little knitting bag clipped to my backpack— yes, I am one of those people who, thanks to the airline policy to spank passengers with additional charges for anything they can think of, defines "one carry-on bag" as a bag that is packed to the point of zipper-busting bulge, and then further enhanced and expanded by sundry items (knitting bag, Vibram Five Finger Toe shoes, a fanny pack) connected via carabiner.

Knitting is good. Knitting is actually our connection to Maine (more on that in a bit). Knitting is a way for me to keep my sanity in this motherfucking line and to hang onto, if only for a few more moments, the sense that I am somehow better and more at peace than those around me because unlike them, I have not (yet) flipped out. *I am so calm!* See how calm I am? I am calm enough to be calmly knitting. I am purling placidly amidst the haste. Lalala... *look at me!* A role model if ever there was one.

And then another hour passes. My back hurts. I am tired of my knitting. The clock is ticking. Warren and I know that even if they were allowing northbound flights out of Newark, which they aren't, still there will be no flight to Portland. All we can hope for is a very early morning flight, one that will allow us to catch our ferry. Toward this end, I get a text message from Continental Airlines— ah, technology!— informing me that I have been rescheduled for a flight leaving at the crack Tony Orlando and Dawn.

I allow myself only the tiniest exhale of relief because a) I don't believe these fuckers and b) even if I really do get a new flight, Warren has received no similar text. So we are staying in this line, this solid, non-moving wall of increasingly crankier people. Testiness tiptoes over to me, creeps in, wraps me tight in its grip. On the bright side, I might just be accidentally starting to cultivate compassion for the cruise ship missers.

Time in airports is so warped— either moving too slow because you're in a hurry to get wherever and there's just been another delay or moving way too fast because you have to catch a connection and you have five minutes to get to another terminal six miles away and the little monorail is broken— that I can't seem to gauge with any accuracy if we stand in that line for one hour or three. All I know is that when we finally make it to the counter, I must remind myself to try not to lose it, to remember that the woman working on the other side of the desk is in a super tense situation, that it wouldn't be nice to add to that, and that if I do, I'll have to make room for her in my head alongside Tia. More to the point, she holds our vacation fate in her hands. Better to be nice. Or at least not a total bitch.

I tell her that I think I'm already squared away with an early morning flight. She types and types and types and types and then says yes, I have an early flight, but it's not until next Tuesday. *NEXT TUESDAY?* This cannot be right. Next Tuesday is two days before I am scheduled to fly home and two days after the hotel on the island closes for the season. TUESDAY? I double-check the text. Yes, in fact, they want to fly me to Maine five days after I am scheduled to fly to Maine. This piques my curiosity and I suddenly find myself wondering why more people don't go postal at airports, why, in fact, they don't call it *going airportal.*

By now we are tired. We are cranky. I no longer wish to lie to myself that I am all centered, and that 24 hours from now none of this will matter. Oh no, I am IN THE MOMENT. The clerk says, "Would you like to fly out at 5 am tomorrow? We can get you on a flight from Newark to Cincinnati, and then three more that will get you to Maine by midnight Friday."

Before I can confirm with Warren what even my geographically- challenged brain knows— that Ohio is West and Maine is East— the agent, looking at her screen, says, "Oh, never mind. Those seats just got taken!" And then she giggles. She *giggles.*

To his credit, Warren is able to convey to me almost instantaneously that this giggle falls under the category of what I call the Funeral Titters. It is not an actual *haha* laugh, as in "I think your fate is funny." It is a nervous laugh that means, "My god this job is nerve-wracking and I hate it and I need to find a new job before somebody lunges across the counter and strangles me." This is good work on Warren's part because after hours of feigned patience, I am about ready to make headline news.

Now Warren and I must confer and, hopefully, concur, and quickly before any next opportunity is lost. This is when he begins to press a little harder with his idea that we just turn around and fly back to Austin. And I resist. And then, just when it's looking like we're heading for the sort of deadlock that's going to prompt one or both of us to say, "That's it, LET'S BREAK UP!!" instead, one of us (I don't even remember which) unleashes a declarative statement that, ultimately, will change our relationship. Forever.

"Maybe we could rent a car and drive to Maine!"

This idea is so harebrained, so preposterous, so beyond the pale that it instantly appeals to both of us. iPhone gets whipped out, GPS consulted, calculations made. We are six hours from Portland. It is 9 pm. Even if we can get our hands on a rental car and track our luggage, we won't be on the road for another hour. At least. This will require driving all night. And then, once we cross into Maine proper, it will require driving most of the day. Truly an insane idea.

We turn back to the nervously giggling airline desk jockey. We tell her sure, book us for a Tuesday flight. Or a Wednesday flight. We don't give a fuck. Just hold us a space. Just in case. In case we come to our senses between now and the car rental people handing Warren a key.

Then we decide to divide and conquer. At least Warren now has his phone and I have mine, so we can communicate. He will go try to find a rental car. I will go try to find our luggage. As I head in the general direction of the baggage carousels, armed with some vague information about some official bag people I need to coerce into tracking my bags, I already begin to formulate a narrative. You have to have a narrative if you want to get to the front of the line. In this case, at long last, I can see a benefit in Warren's diabetes. I'm going to play the, He-Needs-His-Insulin-Or-Else card.

CHAPTER FIVE

*G*am *zu lebracha* is a Hebrew expression, which, more or less, means *This too is for a blessing.* It is the phrase that comes to mind as I wind my way through the increasingly irritated Newark airport crowd and attempt to navigate to the baggage counter. Up until this point I never, ever, *ever* considered Warren's diabetes a blessing. It has taken a visible toll on him. It has made both of us angry— him at not wanting to admit to having let alone having to manage a chronic condition and me, screaming and in tears, begging him to just take his fucking insulin already.

But in this moment? In this moment, *Gam zu lebracha*! I know once I find the right airline rep to talk to, I can explain that Warren left his insulin in his suitcase, and that retrieving it is dire. My between-the-lines message being, of course, "You don't want him going into a diabetic coma on your watch, do you?" This, I reason, will expedite the process of getting our luggage back.

When at last I reach the Counter of Luggage Retrieval Insanity, I am greeted by a woman who has apparently been teleported in from the 1950s as indicated by her up-do, her smear of bright red lipstick, a uniform that seems somehow different than her peers, but above all by her can-do attitude which gives off an air that she is, like Rosie the Riveter, an independent working gal, just happy to be employed! In a sea of miserable, stranded travelers and perpetually grumpy airline employees, she is the sole cheerful person in the Newark airport, possibly in Newark itself.

Inspired and infected by her good attitude, I momentarily revisit the cheerful place I'd been way back when I boarded my first flight, 700 hours ago, that morning, just prior to the post office incident with Tia. Riding this momentary, mini-wave of positivity, instead of broaching the insulin topic in the vaguely threatening, semi-hysterical fashion I'd been rehearsing in my head, I deliver the news calmly and with all politeness. How can I bully a woman who has just arrived here from 1954 and knows nothing of the brusque ways of today's travelers?

The cheerful baggage angel, let's call her Beatrice, nods understandably and smilingly explains to me a retrieval process so archaic that I want to look around for hidden cameras to see if I am an unwitting participant on a new reality show called something like: *Ha Ha! We're Just Fucking With Ya!* Because, according to Beatrice, the "system"— in this otherwise high-tech world, where no other process can take place without someone typing away at a keyboard while frowning at a computer screen for at least a half-hour— is downright Luddite.

Beatrice pulls out a slip of paper and a laminated chart that resembles a cross between oversized placemat— something that might be used in a daycare center to capture widespread Cheerios cast broadly by a toddler— and a picture menu offered to foreign travelers who cannot read the language of the land in which they travel. Pointing to photo images of various styles of luggage, as well as a color chart at the top, she asks me to describe the bag that contains the insulin so she can write down all the details. Of course Warren is traveling with the strangest bag in all of history, something I'd remarked on that morning when I demanded to know where he'd gotten it and why it was shaped that way. He'd acquired it from his dad, a geochemist, who had possibly used it to transport 2 x 3' blocks of geo-samples to conventions, seemingly the only possible explanation for this curious bag design.

While a line builds up behind me, I try to inform Beatrice as best as I can, pointing first to one picture and then another and then yet another. "It's kind of like a combination of these, only the handle is longer and the bag is squatter and…"

Beatrice earnestly jots down a few notes and offers suggestions for the description. "Is it like a pilot's bag, maybe?"

A pilot's bag? Hmmmm. *Maybe.* "Uh, not exactly," I say. I am realizing that, despite her good cheer, we are likely never going to get this bag back. Once she's written down all the info that she can —scrawled by hand on a scrap of paper— Beatrice explains the next step. Eventually a man will come by wearing a vest, she says. He will take the scrap of paper and go to a "huge mountain of luggage," which for some reason my ears translate into "The Big Rock Candy Mountain!" Once the man in the vest arrives at the Big Rock Candy Mountain, he will rappel down it, clutching the scrap of paper with the handwritten description, until he finds what might be our bags. (I'd squeezed in a description of my own, far more conventional little suitcase, conveniently colored teal). Beatrice then tells me I need to "go sit over there"—she points to a spot ten or so yards away from her counter— and "watch for the man in the vest."

I plop down and lean against a pillar and watch for Vest Man while simultaneously fielding a stream of texts from Warren who is over at the car rental counter, trying to negotiate with them, balking at the fee they want to charge him for a 24-hour rental.

Though I am often one to never quit, or at least one who only quits way, way, way past time when normal and even subnormal humans would quit, a sinking resignation floats in and settles over me. I slump further forward and see the ticker tape message scroll across my mind: *Fine, fuck it, let's just take a plane back to Austin or WHEREVER just GET ME THE FUCK OUT OF NEW FUCKING JERSEY because EVERY TIME I come here, even if it's just a goddamned layover, my life goes to fucking shit.*

I text Warren, "We can go back to Austin. Honestly. I don't give a shit. I just want out of this hellhole." As I hit send, in comes a message he must have sent simultaneously: "Car rented. Let the adventure begin (er continue)!"

Warren follows up this text with a phone call in which he is very cheerful. He apologizes for being negative earlier and explains that he had an epiphany: going with me to Maine is totally worth the car rental fee! He's got us a nice new Nissan! We are going to be driving all night! Our dream vacation is going to happen after all!

If, that is, we can track down the teal roll-on and the bizarre geo-sample pilot bag. I tell Warren I need to go have another word with Beatrice. Beatrice, who at long last is starting to show the wear and tear of being perpetually bombarded by a nonstop stream of highly annoyed customers, is a bit harried when I approach her, lipstick and smile both having faded considerably. She wants to know if I've check Carousel Nine yet?

Carousel Nine? *Carousel Nine?*

Then it clicks. I was supposed to check a certain special carousel to see if the man in the vest did his job. I stumble over to Carousel Nine. There, possibly having circled for an hour or longer now, is my little blue-green bag and that utterly bizarre box on wheels that Warren refers to as a suitcase.

Got the luggage, I text him at 8:39 p.m. He zips around to pick me up. This is the start of a very, very, very long night.

CHAPTER SIX

In my twenties, like many people in their twenties, I was a bottomless energy pit. I thought nothing of going out drinking well past the point of mild inebriation, then either heading home for a drunken one-night stand with a bar pickup or (more often) hitting a late night restaurant to shovel mountains of eggs or endless falafels into my gullet before crashing for a few precious hours, and then reporting in, totally hung over and reeking of stale beer, to whatever bottom rung job I happened to work at the time, my employer either failing to realize or care that I was an out of control boozer. (Or maybe my loyalty kept me employed— rare was the day I called in sick, no matter how badly my head was splitting, and always I did my job.)

In my mid-thirties, I quit drinking, in large part because I could no longer bounce back the day after as I once had. I was worn out, woke up exhausted most days. Sobering up re-energized me. Being a single mother came with challenges, but mostly I managed the daily hustle of getting the child to school and extracurricular activities while holding down sundry freelance gigs and upholding my (admittedly questionable) standards of housekeeping. I also ran errands, read books, maintained a rather stunning number of friendships, walked miles every day, and still found time to spend obsessive hours wondering when I might find true love.

More than one summer during these years of abundant energy, I tossed my son in the car and started driving. It was not unheard of for me to drive 500 miles in a day, sometimes more. We might cruise from Texas to Missouri with just one brief overnight stop at a shitty motel in Oklahoma. And then, after visiting Henry's dad and his family in St. Louis, we'd hop back in the car and head to South Jersey to see my people.

I remember one trip, summer of 1999, when Henry was eight, and our vehicle was an '88 Toyota Cressida that had been given to us by some friends. The Cressida had once been stolen, when my friends still owned it, taken for a joyride, and deposited in a lake. It was retrieved and rehabbed, and except for a non-working air conditioner, the thing ran like a top. (Another friend, a hoarder of National Geographics, told me there was an ad in the '88 issues touting the Cressida as having a ride on par with a Mercedes.)

Henry was still young enough to be required to ride in the back seat for safety. It was hot as steamy shit that summer and we were driving our Japanese Mercedes across the Pennsylvania Turnpike, windows down, alternately listening to radio reports of efforts to recover the bodies of JFK, Jr., his wife and her sister and advice and requested tunes doled out by radio host Delilah to the down and desperate. Well, I was listening. Henry couldn't hear much at all, what with the wind whipping at him at 75 mph. Our "conversations" consisted of me shouting some question that would instantly get grabbed and hurled away from us by the velocity-generated wind while he hollered back, *"WHAT?!!"*

I think about those days as Warren and I throw our bags into the trunk and get into our little rental Nissan and prepare to drive all night to Maine, to make it to the ferry in time. Already I am tired. My body, pushing closer each minute to the mid-century point, is no longer the stamina machine of my youth. The prospect of making it to Port Clyde in time looms daunting.

Granted, I feel a small rush at having escaped the inside of that airport full of senior cruise shippers and junior Jesus freaks, and an added boost at the prospect of getting the hell out of New Jersey, sort of an ongoing hobby of mine. But I am not naïve enough to try to fool myself into thinking this will be an easy drive. Counterbalancing my giddiness is the undeniable, unavoidable truth of Warren's circumstances-specific narcolepsy. And yes, one of the main triggers for his sudden naps-without-warning happens to be Getting Behind the Wheel of a Car and Driving More Than Five Blocks.

The rare times I allow him to drive me, invariably I will look over and see him start to nod. And I will say something thoughtful like, "WAKE UP YOU'RE GOING TO KILL US." And eight times out of ten an argument will ensue as he crankily insists he is *not* falling asleep and that I am just randomly criticizing his driving for sport. At which point I will threaten to jump out of the moving vehicle claiming far greater survival odds than if I remain his passenger. And so, over the years, we have come to an agreement that has me doing the majority of the driving, a move that I believe we have adopted in order to stay alive, and he believes we have adopted to shut me up.

There are exceptions to the rule. If we're in the middle of insane traffic in some crazy place with apparently no traffic laws— I'm talking to you, Monterrey, Mexico— Warren will get this gleam in his eye, insist he is driving, and delight in taking the wheel and pretending he is in a video game. He will then shepherd us expertly along what to my eye appears to be a corridor of utter destruction and guaranteed death, roads that either have no center lines or, if they do, these lines seem to be invisible to other drivers. This fills him with obvious glee in equal and opposite proportion to my terror. Warren also far surpasses me in the driving department when it comes to ascending or descending steep, unpaved, single-lane mountain roads that do not come with the benefit of guardrails.

In these challenging, dangerous instances, Warren is Mr. Wide Awake, a double good thing because the very same circumstances cause me to engage in a semi-permanent wince. Excitedly he sits at full attention, ready to be the high scorer in Drive for Your Life while I sit beside him, eyes slammed shut, gripping the Oh Shit Handle above the door, my knuckles whiter than a gaggle of Mormons in a snowstorm. It's as if he has been given a rare superpower by the universe, one that lays dormant for months or even years at a time, but which can be summoned as needed, almost as if all of his car naps were really about storing up the energy required for these scary moments.

But those rare, freaky challenges aside, I do the vast majority of the driving, the long flat stretches, the mundane highways and byways. So I know— or at least I think I know— that as we tuck ourselves into our little rental car on this night, if we are to get to Maine, I am going to have to convince my middle-aged body to pretend it is thirty years younger, to tap into some ancient balls-to-the-wall inner-drive that used to propel me through the world with very little sleep, and pull more than my own weight with the driving duties.

But at least for a little while, until we get past New York City, Warren is in charge, since I get sick just thinking about traversing the Brooklyn Bridge. Not Warren. Warren gets a huge boost contemplating this challenge. Not that we're positive this *is* the Brooklyn Bridge. Despite the fact that he once lived in New York briefly and I've visited countless times, and despite the other fact that we have with us not one but two GPS devices (over which, yes, of course, we manage to argue which is superior), we still wonder aloud what bridge we're on. This is a good and funny way to get the trip going, to realize that we're not even sure if we're on one of the most famous bridges in the world.

One thing we can verify with our naked eyes is that even though it is now 10 pm, these nutty New Yorkers are out driving— crawling actually— like it's rush hour on a Friday. Where the hell do they all come from? Why are they here? Can they not see we are in a hurry to get where we're going? Why in god's name would anyone ever live in this dirty, overcrowded place?

My fear and whining don't stand a chance though, because in this moment, Warren is chipper. No random slumping and snoring right now. Nope. His alter ego— Über Mensch! — has arrived, and I have to admit that, though I'm not usually a fan of cockiness, tonight cockiness is looking pretty good. Cockiness is going to get us past this city.

Observing Warren in this state also summons one of my happiest memories of Us Together, another time ÜM magically materialized before my eyes. I'd taken him to Real de Catorce, a little village in the state of San Luis Potosi, Mexico, one of my favorite places in the world (in fact the place where Warren first demonstrated his ability to drive up mountain roads in a conscious state). We went for a hike in the mountains one day. For as many established paths as there are, there are at least twice as many opportunities to inadvertently wander away from the path. Which is what we did, errantly stumbling down a non-path, bumping into rocks, getting clothes tangled in prickly cactus, realizing at some point that we were heading not toward a rough-hewn trailhead, but instead into someone's backyard.

There, we encountered a couple of horses and a donkey. I was so busy trying to avoid the horses, being a great fearer of horses, that I failed at first to notice the donkey eyeing me as if he needed kick target practice or, perhaps, was craving a delicious hand knit sweater for lunch. When he took an assertive step or two in my direction, a panic rose up in me as if this were a charging bull situation. Before I could scream or faint or hyperventilate, Warren sensed my panic, the way a dog can sense thunder long before humans. He gripped my elbow, and in a deep, growly-but-calm voice, commanded me to, "Just move forward, *now*," then steered me to safety.

The entire event probably took about four seconds. When I replay the movie in my head, though, it's a Spielberg epic with Warren saving the day— not just my life, but the lives of untold others—making Schindler look like a slacker by comparison. So moved was I by that save, by his calm thoughtfulness and grace under pressure, that to this day when I find myself mad enough at him to spit, I'll sometimes call up the memory of that day as a way to settle down, to soothe the fury.

As Über Mensch! guides us over the Brooklyn Bridge (or whatever bridge it is), a new, equally good memory immediately begins forming. I feel deep gratitude that Warren is handling this nerve-wracking task, and this thankfulness deepens as he exhibits an atypical absence of highway hypnosis, staying awake and alert enough to handle driving for a whopping two hours beyond the bridge.

At last, he finally does begin to nod like a junkie, and it is my turn to take over. I see we've covered nearly a hundred miles, nearly one-third of the 324 miles between Newark and Portland, a distance our mapping devices estimate will take us six hours and two minutes to conquer. Once in Portland, we've got to trade out our rental car— this thanks to the fact we'd reserved one in advance and no, the fucking rental car people in Newark could not/would not magically make it so that we could just skip this ridiculous swap and blow on through to the ferry. Then another 88 miles down roads that curve like the twisted intestines of a bloated goat, making the very slow speed limit not something to be challenged (my habit on open highways) but obeyed like an old-school, wimple-wearing nun.

Warren can, personally, go from sixty to zero inside of about forty seconds, and that is the case now that his Brooklyn-Bridge adrenaline burst has given way to the lid-drooping, shoulder slouching, hunch-over-the-steering wheel posture that quietly screams to me, "Prepare to die!" He falls deeply, snoringly asleep five seconds after we switch places. This does not bode well. In daylight I can drive for hours and hours with Warren asleep beside me, an audiobook keeping me company. In the dark of night I need better conversation than a recorded narrator can offer. Without Warren to banter with, I have a feeling I'm going to go down fast.

So much for all those times I bragged about being a truck driver's daughter, and how once I made it 888 miles in a day. On this trip, I make it about thirty minutes before sundry tried and true techniques I've developed over the years— slapping myself in the face, turning up the radio, biting my fingers one at a time, very hard— fail to rouse me. "Warren," I say, waking him up as I pull into a McDonald's parking lot. "I gotta sleep."

To sleep, perchance to dream! Well, okay, to sleep perchance to gather together enough energy to hobble on up the coast and beat our deadline. Here my memory grows fuzzy and there are a number of reasons for this. The main one is that for the rest of the night we will have these weird stop-and-start moments, more than a few of them occurring in McDonald's parking lots. Between the ubiquity and the uniformity of these bright, shiny, plasticky dispensers of fast "food," by the time we get to our second or third one, I can no longer tell if it is the second or third one. Or maybe it's the fourth one.

I have certain habits and memories around McDonald's. I want to say I wouldn't be caught dead in one, but that would be a lie. Warren and I have a pact— when we are on vacation, far away from being observed by anyone we know, we will sometimes wander into a Mickey D's for some fries. Mostly, we do this in airports, and it is a funny game of ours, an inside joke, a nose-thumbing to Michael Pollan and his always-eat-healthy ilk, those doomsayers whose work we read regularly and try to take seriously. But for every hearty quinoa cake laced with chard and gently sautéed in EVOO we've eaten, and for every Greek-yogurt-thickened, kale-heavy green smoothie we've dutifully slurped down, the rare times we do cross a Golden Arches Threshold, we give ourselves over.

For me and my vegetarian leanings— I say *leanings* because, just at Jimmy Carter lusted in his heart, I admit there are days I still crave Filet O'Fish sandwiches, though I fight the urge— this means ordering up a milkshake and fries, and, in the case of road trips, an extra-large coffee. There is no doubt that McDonald's coffee is truly disgusting, but it is also so familiar that the smell and taste of it have a Proustian effect on me, that stinky brown liquid my blue-collar madeleine, a mere whiff of the stuff stirring in my memory a montage of so many other past road trips.

The first time I wake up in a McDonald's parking lot this night, I'm not positive if it's my bladder that beckons me from a contorted-in-the-front-seat semi-slumber, or Warren jostling me, or a carful of loud, middle-of-the-night seekers of *I'm Lovin' It* that pulls in beside us, the inhabitants spilling out and conversing at top volume, no consideration for the possibility that SOME OF US ARE TRYING TO SLEEP OUT HERE.

Whatever the cause— and likely it's a combination of factors— I wake up in a stupor of the sort perfectly expressed on the face of a toddler that falls asleep in her stroller in one place and then, sans explanation, rhyme or reason, comes to in a completely different place. The disorientation is annoying, scary, and unsettling. You just want to be home, in your own bed, with your own blanket, not huddled under three sweaters, attempting the fetal position in a rental car seat that won't go all the way back, beside a World Champion Snorer.

I stumble into the overly lit McDonald's, aware that my disheveled look might likely put the manager on high alert. I wipe the sleep boogies from my eyes as I stand at the counter, dazed. I order one Egg McMuffin, hold the meat, and try not to think about thousands and thousands of beakless chickens nailed to artificial nests, squirting eggs out their shitholes for our mass consumption. I also think how much I love Egg McMuffins, and how back when I still ate meat in my teens, how much I loved every piece o' crap sandwich McDonald's produced (though thankfully I gave up meat before the introduction of the McRib).

I remember my days working at a McDonald's in my carnivorous youth, calling down mountains of extra burgers at the end of the night, a bounty that my coworkers, who also happened to be my roommates, and I crammed into bags, and carried home on our bicycles, and stuffed in the fridge, to be reheated and eaten later, this despite the clearly stated official mandate that all leftovers were to be destroyed and trashed at the end of each shift. *Mmmm, Quarter Pounders, how I loved thee! Big Mac, my hot meaty lover! Mmm...*

Wake up. WAKE UP! Special order is ready. One Egga Muffin as I like to call it— this slurring title ripped off from some comedian so long ago I can't remember his name. "Egga Muffin!" I declare to Warren, who watches me amused. I also order, based on the enticement of a large poster, an impulse item, a frozen raspberry lemonade, shot to perfection by the food photographer but clearly, upon first sip, revealing itself to be a chemical-filled laboratory concoction, one that has never been anywhere in the vicinity of a piece of citrus or a berry.

No matter. Even this fake, disgusting flavor thrills me. *OMG! I am SO EXCITED! I love McDonald's!!* (Don't tell a soul.)

A bathroom break. Back to the parking lot. Ritualistic scarfing down of Egga Muffin. Brain freeze from frozen drink concoction. And now more of that acid rain coffee. I am in heaven. In heaven and also feeling the nastiness already slopping around inside of my stomach. There will be hell to pay. Hell. Starts. Now.

I watch some more late night locals wander into the McDonald's. Why the hell are they up at this hour? Drugs. Surely they must be on drugs, and I don't mean that as one of those expressions middle-aged folks randomly hurl about when describing, with thinly veiled envy, those possessing the youth they themselves no longer can access. I mean it, like, unless you are trying to get to the last ferry in Port Clyde, Maine by 3 p.m. the next day, the only excuse you can possibly have to be at a McDonald's on I-95 at 4 a.m. surely must involve the ingestion of contraband.

CHAPTER SEVEN

Both of us are awake now, exponentially increasing the odds of a petty argument. This is not to say that Warren and I argue every single moment we are both conscious and in one another's presence. But the scenario occurs frequently enough that it has, over the years, become a sort of running joke between us and among our friends. I say *sort of* because not everyone thinks it's funny— some of our friends visibly squirm when we succumb to cranky four-year-old mode. I, too, often fail to find the humor. Warren, however, rarely misses a chance to exacerbate the tension of this bickering by looking at me and laughing. This, in turn and without fail, prompts me to switch into Outrage Mode. His laughter is Pavlov's bell, my protest akin to dog slobber.

Thanks to having spent years together, I have come to understand that on some level, his laughter is the same as my outrage. What I mean is, he grew up in a family where defusing an emotional bomb is accomplished by getting the other guy to crack up, whereas in my family, fury and the silent treatment are tools to be reached for at the point of fever pitch. It's all fine and good to sit here calmly observing this, and actually the observation has helped us argue less frequently, or at least make up more quickly. We've learned to honor and avoid, most of the time, each other's super hot buttons.

But there are still those perfect storm moments— when, say, we've only had five hours of very bad sleep conducted while contorted in the seats of a tiny rental car under the bright parking lot lights of a fast food restaurant— when we forget all we've learned about getting along.

So what argument do we engage in as the sun comes up over Massachusetts or New Hampshire or wherever the fuck we are when the sun comes up? Honestly, I can't even remember. Probably it is something about which exit to take, or counterpoint speculations regarding whether or not the car rental people will make us trade in this little Nissan that has (almost literally) begun to grow on us. Whatever the particulars, the theme is surely the same as it ever was and will be and the execution sounds like this:

One of Us: Blah blah blah, opinion, random thought, opinion.
The Other One of Us: Nunh-uh.
The Initiator: YEAH *HUNH!*
The Protestor: Nunh-*uh*.

Like I said— four-year-old mode. And on this occasion we are four-year-olds that missed naptime and ate four cupcakes apiece. We're tired, we're cranky, we're jacked up on fast food. By the time we get around to revisiting the irritable exchange much later that day— maybe to try to analyze it in hopes of evolving, more likely to fan the fires a bit more to see if we can squeeze anymore bickering out of it— Warren literally won't remember that it happened at all, and so I'll be hard-pressed to stick the landing on the Mat of Righteousness, something I'm usually much better at. Reviving a disagreement that one party can't recall because, he claims, he wasn't really awake when it happened, is tricky business, something that even I (Master of the Fight) have difficulty with.

So, okay, we'll have to chalk that particular argument up to habit and sleepiness and circumstances beyond our control like the weather and the airlines. Whatever the case, sometime not too long after sunrise, and somewhere mid-bickering, we at long last find ourselves at the Portland Jetport.

Inside at the rental car counter, we explain to the disinterested clerk our situation. *Our flight the night before had been cancelled, we rented this lovely Nissan in Newark, we have grown to love the Nissan as if it were the child we never had together, and can we please keep the Nissan for the duration of our week in Maine?*

Too late. Because we parked it in the garage in a Return Car slot, it has already been reclaimed by the cleaning crew, and is being prepared for some other destiny. The clerk hands over the keys to our new luxury ride— a Kia Rio which, we soon discover, has hand-crank windows and manual locks. Really? They still make these features? This tiny red golf cart on steroids—Shitty Shitty Putt Putt if you will— is clearly, despite the low mileage, a piece of crap. It's like we suddenly woke up in 1985 and found ourselves in possession of a Yugo.

No time to argue with the rental clerk, though. The clock is ticking, and loudly. Not only that, but being one of those people who insists on packing as many activities into a day as humanly possible, and then trying to tack on a few more for good measure, I have convinced myself that we can— nay, *must*— still squeeze in a side trip to Swans Island before we catch the last ferry to Monhegan Island. "Must" because I have pretty extreme OCD issues and, long before we even left Austin, I put Swans Island near the top of the Maine To-Do List. And once something makes it onto my to-do list, no matter how unrealistic that goal might be, the idea of not meeting it fills me with tremendous apprehension. Come to think of it, the notion of having to meet a goal at any cost also fills me with tremendous apprehension.

Here is a moment to stop and observe. Raised on a steady diet of severe anxiety throughout my childhood, it occasionally dawns on me that perhaps I set these unrealistic goals not so much to accomplish the goals themselves, but to set into motion the very anxiety that I claim to loathe. If I might now, I would like for a moment to narcissistically quote from a past bit of my own work in which I dissected my need to make bad choices and then repeat them. Said I: *If you grow up in a pile of cat shit, even if it is pointed out to you later in life that living in cat shit is not the healthiest choice, regardless of that fact, every time you get a whiff of cat shit your brain is bound to think, if only fleetingly, "Ahhhh, home!"*

Because there is no territory more familiar to me than anxiety, much as I hate to admit it, it's entirely possible I seek out that which makes me anxious and/or better still, I seek out opportunities to create the anxiety myself. In a perverse way, the latter also feeds my need to feel utterly in control. Thus if I am going to succumb to my "need" to feel anxious, I damn well better have a say in how that anxiety is going to play out.

And so, ticking clock be damned, I will not think of cancelling the trip to Swans Island, which, for the record, is not an island. Or rather, there is a geographical Swans Island, but the place I have in mind is a yarn manufacturer, located on the mainland, beyond Port Clyde, that is known for its amazing woven blankets and also for its hand-dyed yarns. Once upon a time, the company was located on Swans Island proper, and also got their yarn from sheep living there. Though this is no longer the case, their reputation precedes them and no self-respecting fiber fanatic (*c'est moi!*) would miss a chance to check out their operation while up in this neck of the woods.

Begrudgingly I admit that I can understand when Warren voices reluctance about the side trip. Looking at the time and the GPS, even if we encounter no traffic jams or other delays, we are going to be entering the realm of Cutting It Extremely Close. Hell, we're already there.

Warren knows better than to protest with any true vehemence, though. This knowledge is born of both general experience (I'm pretty unstoppable when I set my mind to something) and in this case, extremely specific experience (if the activity I have planned involves yarn, then the activity will be executed, even if I have to do hand-to-hoof combat with four moose trying to put themselves between me and my object of desire).

My real reason for wanting to visit Swans Island is personal—I am hoping to convince myself to lay out a few hundred dollars I don't have for one of their exquisite blankies. I have also attached Greater Meaning to the trip: I am a blogger, back in Austin, for Hill Country Weavers, aka The Yarn Crack House, where I am paid in luxurious yarn for my online duties. I have promised, Suzanne, HCW proprietress, that I would visit Swans Island (she's crazy about the owners and their products) and do a post about my journey. So even if I could set aside my own desire (I can't), I have a backup excuse ready for Warren should he require one. *I have to do it! It's for work!* And, on top of that, yet a second backup excuse: *I called the Swans Island owner! He's expecting us! I don't want to let him down!*

Probably I should've mentioned this whole yarn thing sooner seeing as my addiction to the stuff is what got me hooked on Maine to begin with. Now that the yarn ball is out of the basket, allow me to elaborate. A brief timeline:

1986— Suffering a deep depression in the aftermath of a miscarriage, I take to my bed and announce I will never be getting up again. To help distract me, one of my sisters teaches me to knit. My first project, a scarf, turns out so tightly knotted (anyone can see the symbolism here) I give up the hobby immediately.

2000— Someone in Austin, having heard me wonder aloud if maybe I should try knitting again, leaves an anonymously delivered bag of purple acrylic yarn, aluminum needles and a *How To Knit* pamphlet on my porch. I re-teach myself and begin creating a very long, very wide cross between a scarf and a blanket. I will refer to this project as "the cigarette," since I have decided to try to use knitting to help me quit smoking (which will turn out to work surprisingly well for six years, until I light up again, when it dawns on me that knitting and smoking don't have to be mutually exclusive—well that, and when I also realize my then-husband has decided, without warning, to sashay out of our marriage. But that, as they say, is another story.).

2001— I am obsessed already with this knitting thing and it is not an obsession that will wane. Soon enough, I walk into Hill Country Weavers and discover a world of knitting supplies far beyond acrylic and aluminum—handspun alpaca, polished bamboo needles, intricate patterns. I am doomed financially by this discovery, but I don't mind.

2007— By now, I have discovered *Rowan Magazine*, a UK production that is essentially porno for knitters. This oversized journal is a biannual affair, the subscription includes gift yarn, and the whole thing runs over $50 per year, which somehow seems like less since the price is listed in English pounds.

Filled with stunning photos of ethereal models swathed in impossible-to-knit garments, this magazine does an outstanding job of doing what the best magazines do: convincing readers that if they get the magazine and create the projects, they, too, will look exactly like a borderline anorexic, wrinkle-free, Goth-pale model barely past her adolescence, and that donning the garment will instantly transport one to the White Cliffs of Dover, a seaside resort, a sunny rose garden, and/or the Queen's private quarters for tea and biscuits.

It is inside of one of these magazines that I spot an ad for a weeklong retreat being hosted by Knitting and Yoga Adventures. Knitting *and* yoga? Conducted on an island off the coast of Maine? With seventeen miles of hiking trails along breathtaking cliffs plus gourmet meals as part of the deal? An adventure, then, that is, in essence, a mash-up of five of my favorite activities in life— knitting, stretching, traveling, eating and hiking? *OMG*. This is better than that old Reese's commercial in which peanut butter collides with chocolate. This promises a five-way intersection of sensory gluttony conducted with a group of strangers— an added bonus, since we'll have to be nice to each other the way we don't have to be when we travel with family— all of whom ostensibly share the same loves. Sign. Me. Up.

But, wait… a visit to the website for this outfit reveals that there is but one little hurdle, namely a price tag that easily tallies more than the cost of my first car. Combined with the cost of my second car and, come to think of it, also combined with the cost of one or two other beaters I've owned over the years. More out of reach then, than a stubborn piece of spinach stuck between a pair of molars in a house with no floss.

Rather than be deflated by this reality check, my mind starts cartwheeling around, taking an inventory of past opportunities in life that initially seemed unreachable and how I managed to seize these. Because I have never let a lack of funding stop me from traveling. For all the years I'd been totally broke, I *always* managed to find ways to escape, even if it was only to a dirty little beach a couple of hours away.

Finagle McSchemer—that's me when it comes to plotting pleasurable excursions. Sometimes in the past, magazines picked up the bill, like the time *National Geographic Traveler* sent me on an all-expenses paid road trip, in a brand spanking new convertible, down Pacific Coast Highway, from Monterey to San Simeon, with stops along the way at fancy B&B's and high-falutin' restaurants. Sometimes, also in the past, I used travel vouchers sent to me as a sort of hush money by airline customer service departments upon receiving one of my infamous, 5,000 word letters of complaint regarding one slight or another. On still other occasions, ridiculously generous friends handed over obscene quantities of frequent flier miles, insisting I go wherever I like.

Now, seeing this ad, I am struck by a thought: *I have got to find a way to weasel a spot on this trip.* Already a skilled barterer—having traded my writing skills with my local yarn shop and a tattoo artist, among others in exchange for a mighty impressive stash of high-end fiber and two half-sleeves of permanent gorgeous ink on my arms— I send an email to the Knitting and Yoga Adventures folks, asking if they might consider a trade. If they will let me attend for free, I promise to help with advance marketing and to write a blog during the trip, a little something extra for the participants.

Social media and networking does not, at this point, have such a stranglehold on the world, so my suggestion is unique and intriguing and I get a response fairly quickly. In exchange for blogging, Facebook posts, Tweeting, and outreach to more traditional print publications, I may attend for free.

2008— I did it! I did it! I have scored many wonderful things over the years, but getting invited on this trip feels like being handed a golden ring. Better still, the reality of the trip far exceeds all of my expectations. This marks the beginning of a most fruitful relationship, one that finds me becoming an accidental Monhegan Island pilgrim, returning autumn after autumn for years.

2011—The retreat had been cancelled at the last minute due to lack of registrants, most prospective attendees too spooked by the terrifying economy to shell out the cost. Even though I'll miss seeing my same-time-next-year knitting buddies, I've convinced Warren to come along, and the company making good on the barter, has agreed to put us up on the island for few days. Well, if, that is, we can get to the ferry in time, which we can— I think— just not until Swans Island gets checked off my list.

CHAPTER EIGHT

Inside of Shitty Shitty Putt Putt, I feel perpetually smooshed up against the steering wheel as I slowly race us, 35 mph the posted speed limit most of the way, toward our destination.

The slow driving has its benefits. New England really is a stunning place, and as we creep along I take in details I would miss at 60 mph. Many of the little towns we drive through remind me of the tiny town where I grew up. This harkening back to my Northeastern childhood fills me with a sense of *This Is What I Come From*. The feeling is as unsettling as it is settling, the faintest scratching at the door of Second Guessing, the *tap tap tapping* of an emotional Morse code that, when translated, sort of whispers in a voice seasoned not with regret but curiosity: *What would have happened if I'd stayed in this part of the world?*

Other thoughts that come pouring in involve early Anglo settlers. Who were these people? Is it courageous to travel by rough seas to a foreign land, knowing disease and death at the hands of the natives await? Or is that just plain insanity? And what of the arrogance of believing it is one's duty to proselytize to the locals? They had to have been nuts. Truly.

These thoughts then give way to the traumatic memory of Mrs. Roberta Supercash, my fourth grade teacher. That bitch. Though not a prodigy, I was, at least in the small town where I grew up, pretty far ahead of a lot of the other kids in several subjects. Reading was at the top of the list of areas in which I excelled, and by second grade I had advanced well past the fourth-grade level. This was before gifted and talented programs were in place, and so the solution was to cobble together work for me to do on my own.

By fourth grade, this individual learning curriculum found me assigned to one-on-one sessions with Mrs. Supercash. Sounds all accommodating and forward thinking, right? Well, it wasn't. Being ahead of the others, being singled out like this was actually a liability. Compounding the problem of unwanted isolation for me was the clear fact that, for reasons I could not comprehend then and cannot comprehend even now, Mrs. Supercash seemed to have it out for me.

Do I really think her attitude toward me was malicious? Possibly not. Possibly she came from a background that urged teachers to be strict and harsh. Possibly she just didn't like be handed the task of teaching me separately in addition to her other duties teaching the group. Maybe she just had a miserable home life and took it out on me. Whatever drove her, I can say this about our interactions: that woman left such an indelible mark on me that forty years after the fact, whenever I am in New England, the ghost of her returns to haunt me, this thanks to her insistence that I read a book called *The Witch of Blackbird Pond,* set in 17th century New England, and then deliver unto her a book report explaining the tome.

Not only did I not like being told what to do (a trait that remains with me to this day), I don't give a shit if that book was an award-winner (and it was)—it *SUCKED*. Or, maybe more accurately, it was incomprehensible to me, and she wasn't going to explain it, and my frustration at these things left me to label that book a piece of crap. Additionally, Supercash never explained clearly what a book report was, and in not letting me know what her expectations were, she set me up to let her down.

I don't think I even finished that book. And somewhere in all that mess, Mrs. Supercash, a minister's wife for Christ's sake, flipped out on me and yelled— perhaps this related to the incomprehensible witch shit, perhaps not. I did not take her dressing down lightly. It weighed very, very heavily on me and left me feeling sick to my stomach and terrified of my teacher.

Not long after, when the Barbie-beautiful Miss Richardson, my music teacher, noted the distress written all over my face during my saxophone lesson, she helpfully asked what was wrong. Feeling both relief and guilt—tandem emotional hallmarks I had recently become acquainted with thanks to my First Confession at St. Ann's Catholic Church— I ratted the bitch out. Miss Richardson, outraged on my behalf, confronted Mrs. Supercash.

How do I know this? Because I was then cornered by the menacing minister's wife, who threateningly informed me that I was *never ever* again to do such a thing, OR ELSE. Ah, yes, child abusers posing as elementary school teachers— hello 1970s! (That said, I never forgot Miss Richardson's kindness, and have carried that with me through life, forever advocating on behalf of children who, by virtue of being under 18, seem to inspire in some assholes the notion that children are on this earth to be put down, screamed at, and bossed around.)

For years, I couldn't even walk by any library shelf that housed *The Witch of Blackbird Pond*, such was my Post Traumatic Supercash Syndrome. Finally, I broke down and bought a used copy in my early forties, thinking maybe I could read the fucking thing and break the wicked spell of perpetual anxiety it had cast upon me. So much for home remedies. I couldn't even crack the cover. I banished that ratty paperback from my home and that was the end of that. *Fuck you, Witch of Blackbird Pond!* And, perhaps more to the point, *Fuck you, Witch of Fourth Grade Book Reports!*

So yes, it's a strange thing to be driving slowly through the picturesque, quaint, countryside, here on vacation and seeking out inner-calm, when all the while my monkey mind is jumping around from thought to thought—*Really? Me? A Northeasterner by birth? How did that happen?* and *Fucking pilgrims—you bloody religious nutcase Indian murderers!* and *I wonder if Mrs. Supercash is dead yet? I kinda hope so though on the other hand it might be fun to send her an email and tell her about her lasting influence.*

All these thoughts swirl around yet another background notion, one even further in the recesses: a faint, ridiculous urge to stop and buy a copy of the September Issue of *Seventeen Magazine*, because that's just what you do in the Fall in the Northeast. The temperature and leaves fall and your Pavlovian response is to think about cute kilts and *Five Simple Wardrobe Pieces You Can Turn into 75 Unique Outfits to Last the Whole School Year!* and *How to Make Him Like You Through Lunchtime and Beyond Study Hall!*

Warren nods in and out as I slowly putt-putt us along, my steady 10 and 2 o'clock grip on the wheel not belying the racecar tendencies of my mind. We're both still exhausted from our journey, and, as Robert Frost so eloquently put it, we have miles to go before we sleep. At least the daylight helps rally my energy, as does the promise of a stop at Days Takeout, a lobster shack in Yarmouth, about a dozen miles outside of Portland. Because, yes, me being me, not only have I decided we can cram in a stop at Swans Island, I have also declared we can, should and will be stopping for a quick lunch at this rickety roadside restaurant to fuel ourselves before we continue another mile.

Days Takeout is famous for its lobster rolls, a must have for (almost) everyone who ventures past the *Welcome to Maine* sign. I, personally, am not a lobster person. I tried one once in college, and have had a little bisque here and there over the years. Also, on a previous trip to Monhegan Island, operating under the peer pressure of my fellow knitters (who did not share my qualms about ingesting animals rumored to scream bloody murder as they hit the boiling water) and also operating under a *When in Rome...* rationale (*Isn't lobstering what supports this state?*) I agreed to set aside my squeamishness and, literally, take a crack at eating one of the big red crustaceans. But the tremendous amount of work that goes into getting at the meat— all that cracking and crunching, all that time to think about the ended life of the ancient lobster— confirmed what I already knew: Eating lobsters equaled insurmountable guilt for me. That was my last foray into the arena.

I have no interest in foisting this guilt on Warren. Even if I try, he, a dedicated carnivore, will just wave me off. Instead, I take the opposite approach. Knowing how popular lobster rolls are and how much Warren enjoys trying different foods, I *insist* we stop so he can sample one. This is not really a selfless move on my part. Laugh all you want at my drawing of arbitrary lines here, but despite all I just said about lobster, I am perfectly fine with eating crab. We all have curious food rules, right? Mine just happen to include a claws (ha) that suggests crabs, perhaps because they are smaller, suffer less than lobsters, and so are "okay" to eat. (Please don't challenge me on this for you might win the argument on a technicality, but you will also land yourself on my shit list, and take it from those who have gone before you there, that is not now, nor has it ever been, nor will it ever be, anyone's definition of Happy Place.)

Days has the most bad ass crab rolls in the universe, with crabmeat as fluffy as a recently blow-dried long-haired kitten, flaky as an eccentric aunt, and paler than Snow White after a leeching session. Each little sandwich consists of a mound of this meat and about ninety pounds of hot, melted butter or mayonnaise or maybe both— either way, definitely items frowned upon by the American Heart Association— the whole lot of this crabby, buttery mess piled on top of a toasty warm white hot dog bun.

We're the first customers of the day— an accidental boon of our all-night trip is that we've beaten everyone else here as we partake in an 11 am lunch. We order up one of each: crab roll and lobster roll, plus a Maine Root Beer to split, and head around back to the picnic tables to wait for the staff to a) make fun of us for arriving so early and b) prepare our food. Then I sit back and enjoy watching Warren experience his first lobster roll almost as much as I enjoy experiencing my own crab roll, which, I exaggerate not, moves me deeply. Very, very deeply. As in nearly-to-tears deeply.

Because I am not merely eating a crab roll here, people. I am having an *intense experience.* Just as driving the little winding roads filled my head with a rush of memories, here now comes another wave, this one composed of awe and gratitude: *I am in Maine! I am grown up! I am able to afford delicious food! I am with a man I love, even if we do have our moments! I am on my way to an island to hike and knit and eat and sleep and not answer email!* All of these thoughts, individually and combined, make me want to cry like a freshly crowned Miss America and to jump up and down like a joyful little child in a bouncy house.

I do not ever take for granted occasions like this. Such instances are rare and exquisite, when I have an ecstatic, if fleeting, awareness of being in the absolute present moment as it is joyfully occurring. Then my mind will falter, lose its momentary purchase in the now, tumble back in time, and remember so many hardships of the past—both the sort bestowed upon me by cruel fate and those I brought upon myself. These memories— childhood sorrows, bad men, parenting struggles, brushes with death, financial fiascos, addiction battles— do not dampen my real-time happiness, but heighten it instead. I consider, in a flash, obstacles surmounted, and the wonderful things that fill my life now— time and money to go on vacation, opportunities to see incredible places, great companionship. All this joy mine for the price of a $10 butter-saturated lunch.

I think Warren is a bit less philosophical, but no less enthusiastic, about this culinary delight. He inhales his lobster roll, confirms I did not overrate the promise of it, and announces he's now going back to the window to grab a hot dog because hot dogs are about eight dollars cheaper and now that he's had the delicious portion of the show, he's ready to fill up his tank with good old fashioned processed meat. I fight the urge to get another crab roll, knowing what lies in store for us at dinner on the island, hoping to save some room.

Back in the crappy little Kia, we resume our 35 mph jaunt toward Northport and the Swans Island studio. Technically the digital clock isn't ticking, but it might as well be hooked up to an ominous timpani banging out the seconds and minutes slipping away between now and the final ferry. The GPS is currently predicting it will take damn near close to two hours for us to traverse a mere 80 miles. I push the Kia—*Go, go, go!!* I make a futile attempt to psychically will the tractor in front of us out of the way. *Move, move, move!!* No luck. The tractor takes its time. *Chug, chug, chug.*

By the time we get to Northport, and find Swans Island, we have time for a four-minute tour of the big looms. I get Warren to snap a few shots of me standing in front of the big barn painted with the company logo, grinning big and trying to convey a sense of relaxation, as if I've been there all day as opposed to the reality of the situation. We now have absolutely not even one minute to spare to make it to the ferry in Port Clyde. A single traffic jam will prevent us from reaching our destination and, wise old sayings be damned, sometimes it's not the journey, it really is the destination.

Once again, we are back in Shitty Shitty Putt Putt, without having purchased so much as a single skein of yarn let alone a wildly expensive blanket. We are finally, truly, heading for Monhegan Island. The GPS tells us it'll take just about an hour to cover the 37 miles. That will put us in Port Clyde, at about 3:10 p.m., with twenty minutes to spare before takeoff.

I call the tiny ferry office and tell them we're really coming. The woman who answers reminds me that the boats don't wait for anyone. Of this I am well aware. Maybe my deadline-driven brain, totally warped from nearly thirty years as a journalist, has done this on purpose, waited to see how very close I can cut it. No time to analyze this theory though— must focus on driving.

We have now been on the move for nearly thirty hours since departing Austin. We are going to make that fucking ferry or I am going to fashion our luggage into a goddamn raft and float us over to that island myself if I have to.

CHAPTER NINE

I've said it before, I'll say it again. In my heart, I am a little child. Most often this serves me very well, though other times it makes life difficult. The difficulties usually hinge on anger or disbelief at some unwanted occurrence or derailment of plans. For as bubbly and effervescent as my enthusiasm for life can be when I'm happy, times when I feel hurt, disrespected, pushed away or threatened, my mood can swing out equally in the opposite direction, to the edge of negative hyperbole and beyond.

Black and white thinking and its attendant reactions— please, don't call these tantrums unless you really want to see what tantrum looks like— can, I know, make me sometimes come across as terribly immature. Not the best position to be in when wading through a lovers' spat or fighting the urge to give into road rage or having to wait for something I don't want to wait for.

On the other hand, having the outlook of a four-year-old can be really handy— see aforementioned enthusiasm— especially on vacation. In Buddhism, viewing the world with *beginner's mind* is about approaching life with a sense of wonder, as if you are encountering everything for the first time, leaving you to marvel at even the most mundane objects and occurrences. *This* is why I travel. Because even though I nurture my sense of wonder on a daily basis back home, and even though I can find something brand new on every walk I take along the same path in my neighborhood day after day, you can't help but have a little static set in when you adhere to routines. Getting out there in the world is a reminder to keep open eyes, ears, nostrils, taste buds, hands.

Stop and stick the roses in your ears, run your fingers over the thorns, bite into a velvety red petal.

Warren is the kind of traveler who almost always prefers to go someplace new to him. Not me. I do like new experiences, but I also love circling back and revisiting destinations I love best— Monhegan Island, Maine; Astoria and Portland, Oregon; Real de Catorce, Mexico— I experience a twofold delight: the comfort of familiarity combined with the joyful surprise of witnessing changes that have occurred since my last visit.

Returning also brings a certain sense of belonging. Though I'll never be a local, and though I might not ever be fully accepted by the locals, I will recognize them, and they me, and this incites a soaring sensation— excitement that I am both known enough to be warmly welcomed back, and unknown enough to not accidentally get tangled up in any local drama that might be going down.

The closer we creep toward Port Clyde, the more thrilled I become. True, I'm still exhausted. I'm also totally wired, feeling like I'm coming down from a three-day bender. I can't wait to get back to the island. And *I CAN'T WAIT* to show Warren the place. I know, I know— better to not have expectations and best not to instill them in others. Because how could any place, any person, any dish ever live up to such constant building up, the way I've built this place up for him through my endless stories?

But I know— *I know, I know, I know!!!!*— Warren is going to fall in love with this island just like I have! I know this has to be true because I *want* it to be true. I know it, too, because I felt the same way about Real de Catorce, when I took him there not long after we met. He was as smitten with that little village as I was the first time I set foot there. I was right then and I'm sure I'll be right now.

Cue the *Theme from Rocky*— we arrive just before 3 pm and hustle down to the dock, dragging our luggage. Today we'll be riding over on the Elizabeth Ann, one of two small ferries that make regular runs from Port Clyde to Monhegan Island. The Laura B is the other, and she's smaller and older and slower than her sister ship. Not that EA is on par with the Love Boat or a racing yacht. She's still a small vessel and we'll be riding her across a wide span of ocean— twelve miles might not sound like much, but trust me, you have a sense out there on the water that if that boat goes down you are not going to be successful in swimming safely to one shore or the other.

My hope is for a calm trip across. I am wiped out to the point of feeling sick, sick the way you feel at the end of the day of a severe hangover. There's a great hope in that particular feeling of ill, because you realize you're still alive, and if you can just hang on for a few more hours you will get to sleep, to really sleep, and that you will sleep very hard and the unspeakably delicious sense of rest that will visit you after so much unrest will feel so ecstatic you will almost want to torture yourself again with more sleep deprivation, just to score the reward of more deep sleep somewhere down the line.

Though the thought that bedtime is nigh thrills me, and though I am letting go of the ticking-clock anxiety that ate at me all the way to Port Clyde, this is not the same as feeling calm and relaxed. Actually I feel stretched to my absolute limit. If a gull hovering over the deck looks at me funny, I might have a breakdown. If spray from the boat's wake hits me the wrong way, I might start screaming.

And if the sea is choppy it's going to majorly suck balls. This is not mere theory. My very first visit to Monhegan Island included a trip back over to Port Clyde on the Laura B that was so terrifying that it is a testament to the wonders of the island that I ever returned.

Here I must pause and tell you about my father's attitude toward hurricanes and also about that of a particular birding enthusiast who runs rampant on Monhegan Island at precisely the same time that the knitting retreat occurs each year. Though I didn't even meet the latter until after the former had died, their opposing viewpoints about certain weather conditions tugged me in opposite directions in 2008, alternately convincing me I would be fine and then, no, wait a minute, actually I was going to die.

First, my father. Every summer of my youth, he and my mother would take us nine kids for weekends down the Jersey Shore, where they'd built for us a sheetrock box of a summer house on a tiny island called West Wildwood, a place so small you couldn't always find it on a map pre-Google. The house had beds in most every room, including both kitchens (upstairs and down) to accommodate the eleven of us. The island was, I like to joke, actually below sea level. Well, close enough. With every full moon the streets flooded. With every hurricane, the place turned into a low-rent Venice, with islanders paddling along the newly formed, shallow canals in otherwise unseaworthy vessels.

These hurricanes seemed to come nearly every summer, and without fail they fell during out annual two-week vacation, which was always scheduled to coincide with August 15th. That date, for Catholics, is a Holy Day known as the Feast of the Assumption, commemorating the alleged full-body ascension of the Virgin Mary into the heavens. Believers hold that on this occasion the water is blessed and that all who immerse themselves will benefit. Every summer, thousands of believers— including my parents and us kids— would make the pilgrimage, step into the salty tide and wait for a miracle, which in our case might be as minor (yet seemingly monumental to us kids) as getting through our entire stay without our father flipping out, screaming, and sticking a homemade For Sale sign in the front yard.

Stormy weather was no excuse not to get in the ocean. I swear I have this memory of my father swimming out into the ferocious choppy sea one particularly harsh Feast Day, lighting crashing all around him. Didn't matter. He was duty-bound to God. Or maybe having nine children would make anyone want to swim out far past the lifeguard's limits in a storm.

Hard to pinpoint precisely what led my father to believe he was storm-proof, but this stance extended beyond dangerous swims and included remaining in the sheetrock house, which would shudder and shake violently in the 100+ mph winds that howled around the island with the arrival of each new hurricane. As surely as other families have their own unique annual traditions, we had our Storm Dance, a series of complicated rituals that occurred in preparation for the "holiday" known as landfall.

The house was furnished in Early New Jersey Cast-Off, pieces plucked curbside from the homes of others who'd felt the chairs and couches had been used passed their expiration date. Not my father, who knew a trash-picking bargain when he saw one. All of these unique, well-worn pieces would need to be elevated as soon as the meteorologists' sounded the warning that a hurricane was on the radar.

I wish we had photos from those days, but no one thought to document chairs set up on cinderblocks, ratty old rolled up rugs balanced atop them, the whole of this mock totem pole like a sad little circus of inanimate performers waiting, worriedly. to see how high the water would rise. If it got beyond their legs, crept up to the sagging undersides of seats pre-worn by previous owner/occupants, then off to the curb they'd go again, this time likely for good.

Once the furniture had been dealt with, the next step in the Storm Dance resembled an angry call-and-response, with tremendous underpinnings of terror and anxiety for us kids. There was a lone ambulance on the island, and as the storm whistled in, the driver would slowly cruise the streets and announce over its loudspeaker, "Everybody off the island. This is an evacuation. *YOU MUST EVACUATE THE ISLAND!*"

Invariably, my father would mutter-growl, "We are not leaving this island. Everybody—*UPSTAIRS RIGHT NOW.*" And so up the stairs we'd run, nine terrified children and my mother. We had no TV for many summers, probably not until the late '70s, and even then it was a tiny screen, black and white, and cable service was a long ways off, so at best we might get one or two staticky stations. Mostly though, we had to rely on board games and each other and our father's volcanic emotions to entertain us. Well, these things and a sense of wonder—as in: *"I wonder if we're all going to die tonight?"*

We never did die. The storms would bang and clatter and batter. The house would stay standing. And then out would come our leaky little boat, the one kept next to the house beside the big oil barrel in which rested the crappy, sputtering engine the men were always tinkering with to no avail, as blue-gray clouds of gassy exhaust fumes spat in their faces and across their bare or wife-beater-clad chests. My older sisters would roll up their pant legs, descend the stairs, slosh past the water-logged furniture and wade out to the boat to take it for a float, while we younger kids, envious, were stuck inside and upstairs, doomed to still more mind-numbing rounds of checkers.

Though my father went to his grave without us ever resolving our lifelong mutual disdain for one another, and while I wince at the thought of giving him much credit for anything, I have to admit I have some indefinable emotion, one tinged with a whiff of gratitude, for what he "taught" us about hurricanes. Any therapist – hell any *human* with no credentials beyond basic commonsense— could correctly tell you that what he did to us those summers was insane, unfair, and wrong: You don't put little children at risk like that. But an odd side effect of being forced to ride out those terrible storms is that I have harbored a fascination with hurricanes ever since my childhood, and will watch coverage of one like I'm watching the Super Bowl.

This was what I was thinking the first time I visited Monhegan Island, in late summer 2008. A few days into my stay, I became uncomfortably aware of a regular presence in the living room in the lobby of the Monhegan House. I'd be eating breakfast, or dinner, or knitting with the group, and a nervous man would tromp up the front porch steps, burst into the living room, and stamp over to the old fashioned, corded phone. Cell phone service is limited even on a good day on Monhegan— your best shot at a strong signal is to stand at a high point near the cemetery— so this is one of the few places you'll still find folks relying on landlines as a primary means of communication.

Without bothering to lower his voice, this man, whom my knitting group eventually came to dub Birdman, would, with increasing alarmism, tell whomever was on the other end that we were *going to die* if we didn't GET OFF THE ISLAND NOW. He was referring to incoming warnings of a hurricane, the first to be forecasted for Maine landfall in seventeen years. You know all those movies with all those scenes where someone slaps someone else because they are freaking out and there's no other way to calm them down? His panic made every one of those slapped characters seem calm by comparison, and I'm talking about *before* the slap.

Each time I eavesdropped his latest report, I flashed back to my childhood hurricane seasons ridden out in West Wildwood. By now, I had hosted my Galveston friends more than once for extended stays in my Austin home, thanks to Hurricanes Rita (2005) and Ike (2008). And we had all seen the devastation of Katrina. So my romanticized notion that I could ride out any storm had been tempered quite a bit by the fallout of these more recent and brutal storms. And yet still, I was fighting an urge to dismiss Birdman's commentary because I was my own living proof that one could survive a hurricane— could survive many.

And besides, Birdman was a birder for crying out loud. An über geek. I first caught sight of a group of birders early in the week, during dinnertime. As I sat with my fellow passionate knitters in the Monhegan House dining room, all of us laughing and having a big time, we were unceremoniously interrupted by a flock of humans that tromped in and observed us as if we were statues or subjects on the other side of a two-way mirror, unable to see or hear them.

They did not whisper conspiratorially, but talked loudly among themselves, rather surprising given they had trained themselves to contain outbursts of excitement when out twitching, lest they scare off their fine-feathered friends. As they studied us with our knitting needles and yarn, so we observed them— decked out in safari vests, binoculars around their necks, weighted down with mammoth cameras, their matching ensembles uniforms that cried out WE ARE DORKS AND PROUD OF IT! And then in a humorless tone and sans irony, one cried out, gesturing at *us*, "Why in the world would anyone take up such an odd hobby?!!"

On consequent trips to the island over several years, I would come to dance across a spectrum of emotions regarding these birders: mockery, loathing, irritation, amusement and, finally a cheerful, semi-begrudging respect. But on this, the year of the hurricane landfall, I was gaining my very first exposure to birders in action. And as one might meet a lone Parisian in Arkansas and, depending on this person's traits and characteristics, form an sweeping opinion of the entire population of the City of Light, Birdman's frequent freaked-out lobby phone calls about our impending death did little to nothing to endear him and his flock to my increasingly nervous heart.

Our last scheduled day on the island that year of my first retreat, a Saturday, also happened to be the day meteorologists predicted the storm would touch down, likely on the mainland. By Friday evening I was wondering if I should get up pre-dawn and catch the earliest ferry, before the storm made passage back dangerous, impossible, or— thank you, Birdman— possibly deadly. Inside me my own storm brewed. Should I channel my father and stay on the island and return at my regularly scheduled time, "knowing" I would somehow be safe? Or should I cave to the growing fear inspired by Birdman and get the hell off the island as soon as possible?

My father won out. As luck would have it, as I boarded the Laura B for the return journey loaded down with ginger candy purchased at one of the few stores on the island— ginger supposedly having stomach settling properties to fend off seasickness— I discovered that Birdman, whom by now I was referring to as *Alarmist* Birdman, was along for the same ride. In the end, both my father and Alarmist Birdman were right, sort of. We did survive but that was the worst boat ride of my life, with massive swells rising up and tossing the little ferry like the opening scene from *Gilligan's Island* on steroids.

In the back of my mind— well, okay, more towards the front of my mind— I contemplated human fallibility. I'd seen *The Perfect Storm*, and I recognized that an ounce of hubris or ignorance could, literally, sink our ship. It was an inner voice that increased in volume whenever Birdman started yapping again about the storm, or yet another swell tossed us, or whenever I glanced at a laminated newspaper article tacked to the wall titled *The Venerable Laura B.*

but which, to my nervous eyes, appeared to say *The Vulnerable Laura B.*

Now, boarding the Elizabeth Ann with Warren for my fourth trip across to Monhegan, I think about that first trip back to the mainland. That really was a serious storm we came through, not some fish tale that took on bigger, scarier proportions after the fact. The ship's crew concurred— that was the last trip of the day, the sea deemed to dangerous for the afternoon run.

In the mid-90s, *National Geographic Traveler* sent me on assignment to go to snowboarding camp at Mount Hood, in Oregon, where I was far better at observing boarder culture than I was at staying vertical. After one long, hilarious day on the mountain, spent mostly on my ass, I went with the instructors down to a bar in town where snowboarders threw back beers and watched surf movies.

These coaches were hardly pussies— most of them had broken lots of bones over the years, including their backs, only to get back on the mountain, apparently fearless. And yet one boarder, as he watched the surfers on the screen, said to me he just didn't know how surfers do what they do. The ocean, he explained, is so much more dangerous than an icy mountain, so much less forgiving than snow. The medium is forever moving, forever unpredictable, forever more deadly. His observations always revisit me when I am about to get involved with an ocean.

This time is no exception. I pray (in my own way) for calm passage. My prayers are answered. Less than an hour later we are across safely. In just under an hour, Maine proper seems a thousand miles away, the rest of the world further still. Land ho! There is the shoreline: Monhegan Island. Though this is only my fourth trip to the island, I very much feel like I am coming home, as if I belong here, and have belonged here for centuries. As if I might (happily) never leave.

CHAPTER TEN

Just as we are about to disembark, I spot her.

"Andrea?" I call out, fishing around in my mental Rolodex for her name. I suck with names.

"Angie," she corrects.

"Right. Sorry!"

Angie— whom I first met the year before— is one of those people you don't need time to analyze to ascertain she is someone you want on your team and, perhaps more importantly, someone you do not want opposing you. A head turner with a palpable air of mischievous trouble, she is not mean but quite frank, and you recognize immediately the wisdom in not pissing her off.

Angie is short and solid, olive-skinned, with pronounced, expressive eyebrows and this long, thick, wavy hair— a rich black, prematurely streaked with gorgeous skunky white streaks. Her vocal cords sound as if strung with gravelly beads, and the sight and sound of her combined with the essence of her very being emit a charisma that suggest she could talk her way into— or out of— any number of scenarios. As it happens, her current gig is waiting tables in the Monhegan House dining room, serving breakfast early and dinner late and doing who knows what— *napping? drinking? reading? knitting? screwing?* — in between.

The very first time I saw her carrying food from the kitchen, the sight of her balancing a heavy tray had a time-machine effect, hurtling me back to my own, long-gone, fifteen-year history of waiting tables and answering to tourists. A misty montage flickered across memory's screen and I swooned, not for Angie, but for those days when slinging hash and booze was my happy lot in life.

From my friends who attend AA, I learned about a concept known as *euphoric recall*. The idea is that when you are sitting around in your sobriety, wistfully fantasizing about the good old days of getting wasted, and when your mind settles on a particularly delicious memory of hanging out in the bar one night, getting plastered, flirting, perhaps picking up the guy on the next stool over, you can get very caught up in a romanticized version of what was. At this point, you then have a certain duty to self. Once you are past remembering the drinking and the fucking and the perceived happiness, you must continue the memory to its real-life finish and also recall the puking, the nearly setting your mattress on fire while smoking in bed, the forgetting of the name of the naked person beside you, the STDs you contracted— all those reminders that really, *no really*, quitting drinking was the right choice.

I mention this because, though I have remained sober for the better part of a dozen years, and though the euphoric recall device has helped me to keep the booze at bay, I find it is far less helpful a technique when it comes to another weakness of mine: romanticizing restaurant work. Because while I truly can still remember when I finally burnt out for good— working at the Old Oak Café, resenting even my nicest customers, wanting to pour scalding coffee in their laps not because they did anything wrong but just because I just couldn't take it anymore— once a bit of time had passed, I readily clung to (still cling to) the parts of the job I liked.

George Burns has a quote about how a big, tight-knit family is a great thing to have— in another city. This nod to dysfunction is one I've always found both hysterical and utterly accurate. But it reminds me of a greater truth: we may ditch our dysfunctional families of origin, flee them and leave them far behind, but we will, soon enough, recreate them using nearby substitutes for stand-ins. Nowhere is this more true, I think, than in restaurant work.

Oh how I loved the dysfunction, the drama, the *telenovela* plot lines that unfolded. How I loved the drinking (before and after shifts, *during* shifts). The bellyaching, the affection, the backstabbing, the in-fighting. All this, with free meals thrown in. Plus, not to say waiting tables isn't hard and doesn't involve thought, but really good food workers can, as needed and desired, go on auto-pilot, zone out, work hung over and save their brains for outside-of-work pursuits in a way that many workers — corporate culture drones constantly checking Blackberry devices, teachers grading homework on the weekends— seem unable to.

So when I see a restaurant staff, especially one that is obviously close-knit, and when I discover a waiter like Angie, clearly a leader and not a follower, out the window go the bad memories of my waiter life. I forget about aching wrist and knee joints, dickweed customers, shitty managers, asshole owners. I zero in on the fun memories and cannot follow through and temper these with the accompanying bad truths. In some ways, though I long ago stopped saying, *"If I have to, I can always go back to waiting tables,"* there is a part of my mind that I cannot untrain, cannot convince to understand the folly of yearning for those underpaid days of relying on tips and drinking myself silly every night.

Angie embodies what I loved about waiting tables— her easy manner, her spunkiness. As we step off the boat I hear her talking to another worker who's come down to the dock to greet her. Yes, she says, she ran the errands. Yes she has the sundry bottles of booze everyone ordered. And the smokes. She's both mule and muse, procurer of party goods and, soon enough, center of that party. She's the bad girl and the pretty girl whose beauty lies not in the convention of long golden tresses, slim hips and a Barbie rack, but instead in an exotic air, a smudgy, dark mystery. I could spend my entire week following her around like a puppy dog, sucking up a vicarious thrill, listening in on the island gossip, revisiting my youth.

Warren and I, now truly ready to drop— the heaviness of our exhaustion made heavier by the knowledge that at long last we truly are within countable moments and footsteps of a wonderful bed— summon from our deepest reserves a last half-ounce of energy to look around and get acclimated. We are here, *at long fucking last*, on Monhegan Island, and I, for one, want to weep dramatically, as if I have just returned to my homeland after forty years of exile, as opposed to being on my annual vacation. Warren is excited, too. We wait for the deckhands to toss our luggage into the pile.

The trucks— three of them— have come down to greet us. One of the many points of joy for me here is that there are so few motor vehicles on the island they total in the single digits. A few of the lobstermen have trucks, and a few of the lodgings do, too, to haul supplies and luggage up from the dock, and trash and luggage back down again. Beyond these and the occasional golf cart, island transport is all about self-propulsion. Even bicycles are a rare sight here— these dirt roads are traveled most often by foot.

The crunch of pickup tires on gritty dirt wakes me up. So does the salt air. Every one of my senses is overwhelmed, in fact. The boats, the traps, and the water stretch out in one direction. A handful of familiar shops and galleries dot the road before me. We extract our bags from the dockside heap and throw them in the bed of the truck bound for Monhegan House. I tell Warren to come on, and we begin the little trek up to the old four-story building that, the very first time I laid eyes on the place, called out to me: *You belong here.*

If they ever legalize human/building marriages, I will happily vow myself to Monhegan House until death do part us. Built in 1870, the place is sturdy, covered in weather-beaten wooden shingles, and has a magnificent porch dotted with big, snowy white rockers that silently trumpet the news: *We don't give a shit how important or busy you are off the island, because now that you're here you are going to sit your uptight ass down and relax even if we have to rock on over there and grab you ourselves.*

You step up the two stairs, then take two more eager steps across the porch to the front door, and then cross the threshold into two adjacent, cozy living rooms, the second of which is where you'll find the little office window, behind which— unless he's off running errands or pulling strings behind scenes (as he often is)— you'll find Holden. Holden has these rosy Campbell Soup Kid cheeks that belie his middle age. With his blonde hair and blue eyes and big, deep laugh and stout stance and endless island knowledge, he is a cross between a retired surfer dude, a bouncer, a teddy bear, and an air traffic controller. He is also the personification of a lengthy Wikipedia entry about the island.

Holden's wife, Sue— petite, efficient, twinkly, observant and, I'd wager, not one who suffers fools gladly— co-captains this ship. Between them, they make sure guests feel fully tended to, and that nothing is ever wrong, or that if it is, that resolution is imminent. They also manage to be extremely friendly without crossing that invisible line that might let an occasional fussy guest take advantage, manipulate or whine too much.

This is yet another part of the trip I love— watching Holden and Sue in action. Because in addition to fifteen years of food service, I also put in my time starring in the real life movie *I Was a Teenage Chambermaid at The Hotel Muy Grande in Wildwood Crest, NJ*. There, under the none-too-benevolent dictatorship of a former beauty queen named Juana— who loved to march around, snapping her fingers and pointing while proclaiming, "DETAILS!!"— it fell to me to literally clean up the shit of others, shit they could not always be bothered to get into the toilet. Hospital corners on sheets, restocking towels, running the vacuum, scrubbing the tubs— all these underpaid tasks gave me privy into people's oft-unpretty habits and the inner workings of hotel management.

I love this, too, about traveling, how one experience begets a memory of another, and how they all overlap to create a tangle of feelings that cross back and forth across time and locations. Trying to sort through would be like attempting to untangle a magnificently soft hank of lace weight yarn that the cats had had a go at. But so what if you can't separate them out, one from another? It doesn't matter. The process is the payoff, senses fully engaged.

And so on Monhegan Island, I float from what is happening, right in front of me, off to some faraway time when I wielded a toilet brush to earn my meager living, and the magic of the place allows me to romanticize even that mundane and genuinely shitty job. The ancient, buried knowledge of cleaning up after strangers rushes to the surface in vivid detail whenever I pass a young maid in the hallway, lugging a vacuum or carrying an armful of fresh white sheets. Though I don't feel quite as wistful for hotel maintenance as I do for waiting on tables, still, an odd nostalgia presents itself and a fleeting fantasy fills me. Wouldn't it be fun and amazing and earth-shaking to give up my life in Austin and beg Holden and Sue to hire me on to do anything at all that would allow me to stay here?

Do I really want to help run a guesthouse on an island packed with tourists in the summer and kooky birdwatchers, knitters and landscape artists in the fall? Hell no. But Holden and Sue make doing so seem not exactly easy, but possible. Possible and very, very interesting.

Maybe what I yearn for most is the ability they have to conjure up a kind of magic that gives guests an experience so wonderful that, months later, in the dead of winter, when they are sitting in their godforsaken little gray cubbies out in godforsaken Little Gray Cubbyland, their minds will drift, sans explanation or warning, to a memory of Holden laughing or Sue seating them in the dining room, and the whole adventure will come racing back, momentary blissful respite from the Sisyphean tasks of answering incoming emails, navigating rush hour, and other drudge responsibilities of life.

I introduce Warren to Holden and Sue. Holden and I engage in a little bit of insider talk about the cancelled knitting retreat, immediately dispensing with small talk, falling into the conversation like siblings at a family reunion. Yet another plus of annual pilgrimages comes thanks to an unspoken, *Same Time Next Year* agreement. Each year, after one week together, we will all go our separate ways and spend fifty-one weeks apart during which we will have little or no contact with one another. Then we will reunite and start talking right where we left off, as if an hour, not twelve months, has passed.

I ask about the birders— yes, they are here in full force, and yes, of course, Birdman is in the lead. Over this we have a good laugh. After that first terrifying year of having the bejeezus scared out of me thanks to his hurricane alerts, I begrudgingly and tentatively came to first accept and then genuinely like Birdman over the next two years. Last year, especially, had been hilarious. He'd agreed to come to our final night party, and was a good sport about being the center of a mini roast we held in his honor, complete with a little knitted bluebird I'd affixed to my head and which I had "flown" toward his head.

Holden tells us our room number and we head for the stairs, promising to be back down for our 6:15 dinner reservation. He doesn't hand us a key— there are no locks on the doors here, just little hook and eye latches on the inside, which are not about safety but holding the door tight against windy ocean gusts dancing through the windows.

Ascending the narrow staircase ratchets my happiness quotient even higher. The French have a saying, *L'esprit de l'escalier*, which translates to *the moment on the stairs*. Technically, this is an idiom referring to how, so often, we think of a witty retort to a stupid comment when it's too late to deliver that remark in a timely fashion. You know, like when you're leaving a party and it dawns on you the perfect thing you should have said to your partner's ex, whom you ran into, and who said something catty, leaving you momentarily mute.

For me, *L'esprit de l'escalier* takes on a literal significance at the Monhegan House. Just as Angie and her waitress tray hurtle me back across time to my own days slinging hash, and the towel-toting maids transport me, too, this staircase also has magical properties. Only in this case, I am not traveling to any real time I can recall in my personal history. Instead, I'm haunted with a déjà vu, as if I have been here before, and by before I don't mean the last year or two. I mean I am filled with a very real sense that I lived on this island and worked at this house in the 1800s.

Preposterous, right? I mean, even with all of my Buddhist aspirations, the one part I truly can't wrap my head around conceptually is the whole reincarnation thing. Do I really think I was a princess or a handmaiden or a lap dog or a warrior in a past life? Nah.

But I swear that, whether I am creaking up or creaking down those steps, a part of my soul has been here before. Perhaps there is a simple, plausible explanation for this related to my childhood summer pastime of devouring *Little Women* and the rest of Louisa May Alcott's work. I was fanatical about reading and rereading these 19th century tomes, the escapism they offered priceless, delicious, and necessary to my emotional survival.

Lost in a sea of nine children, perpetually squashed down by my constantly enraged and consistently unreasonable father, I took more than a little solace in the lives of the March girls. Those books lulled me, anchored me, calmed me. I so inhabited the world of Jo and the rest of them that it's like a part of me entered that book, the way Gumby used to walk into books with his pony pal Pokey. Perhaps I was a doily upon the chair arm of the grumpy aunt, or maybe I was a schoolmate of little Amy. A peripheral character, whoever I was, but still a player even if only a bit one.

Seeing as the whole *Little Women* deal went down in New England in the 1800s, is it any wonder then that this staircase in this rooming house built in 1870 on this island off the coast of Maine, in New England... well can't you see then how every time I step upon it something inside of me aches like I belong? Like I am stepping *into* something rather than merely accessing an upper or lower floor?

In the Haggadah, there is a section about how God did one great thing and then another, and that these things, each individually, would have been sufficient. Hell, there's a whole fifteen-verse song sung at Passover about it—*Dayenu!* (which translates, more or less, to *enough* and which, shortened to *day*— pronounced DIE— curiously is also how you say the equivalent of *shut up* in Hebrew, by screaming, "Die, die, die!!" at the person you wish to silence.) But God just keeps going, giving more.

This is how I feel about the Monhegan House. Though I swear I could satisfy myself spending all my time here traipsing up and down the stairs, holding imaginary conversation with LM Alcott, I am also eager to move on. Because I know the prize that awaits us. Yes, that's right. There's more. Our room at the top of the stairs. And this I also cannot wait to show to Warren.

Do you know this painting, *La Chambre à Arles*, by Vincent Van Gogh? The work depicts a simple little bedroom: small bed, wood floors, two chairs, a little table, a few pictures, a window, three clothes hooks, and a towel. This is one of my favorite Van Gogh works— one of my favorite paintings, period— representative of a simplicity I crave, a craving that increases each year as the world gets busier and more connected and less easy to tune out and step away from.

Twenty-eight variations of this very room exist at The Monhegan House, the simplicity of the space perhaps the biggest draw of all. Our room is centered by one big white bed, a cloud upon which floats smaller clouds: heavy comforter, marshmallow pillows, sheets crisper and whiter than matzoh. The electric lighting is minimal— an extension cord snakes out from the sole outlet near the door and slithers around the perimeter of the room, powering a tiny lamp, light dim enough that if you plan on doing nighttime reading you'd best bring your own book light.

There are the towels, also white, nothing fancy, just clean and functional. There are few hooks upon which to hang them after use. There is a simple dresser, with drawers that expand and stick in the moist and salty air, requiring a hearty tug for full access. This damp air, a discernible cold bite to it, blows in through the open windows. At home I would close windows and doors to such a chill. But we have just traveled from a place in the midst of what will soon officially become labeled the hottest summer on record, a time also of the greatest drought ever recorded in Texas. Despite my preference for heat over cold, my insistence on living in the south, right now this cold air is a life force, and the moisture in it a novelty, something I'd forgotten was possible. Thrill, delight and calm all jockey to get to the front of the line of emotions that rush in as I look around.

"Isn't it fantastic?" I ask Warren.

That sounds rhetorical, to be sure, but I also want an answer from him, maybe an eager whoop, maybe just a grin of appreciation, something to reassure me that he loves this place, too— less because I want him to be happy (though there is that) and more because I want to know that my partner shares this appreciation for simplicity. Because if I take a moment to pull myself out of this giddy stupor of mine, I can remember that somewhere there are travelers out there who would not appreciate the stripped down, bare bones spectacular nature of this space. I have even met people like this— who would turn up their nose at what, to their mind, would appear to be a dearth of amenities. The lack of television, the poor cell phone reception— these are the sorts of things I would gladly pay extra for.

Because this space here, with its blank slate potential, says to me several things I most wish to hear but don't hear nearly often enough: *Your job in this room is simple— you must sleep the sleep of the dead to the tune of a salty breeze and a rhythmic tide. You are safe here, far from meetings and corporations and Big Box insanity. Your options are limited and sometimes that is the very best thing any of us can hope for. Shhhh.... Shhhh... come now, lie down. Sleep.*

My waking life off the island is hectic. Less so than it used to be back in the days of my son's soccer insanity, his need to be driven to school, my need to work for others to make a living. All that has changed now and technically I have a lot more time. I only ever wake to an alarm if I have an early flight to catch. And yet despite these changes, both organic and planned, sometimes I fear that I have lived so long in Deadline Mode that, these fleeting trips to Monhegan Island and a few other places aside, I will forever be stuck in Anxietyville.

For example— whereas in the old days my daily to-do list might have included seven parenting duties, three writing deadlines, a dentist appointment, grocery shopping, and a trip to the vet's to get the dogs' anal glands expressed, these days it looks more like this: yoga, long walk, one or two half-hour client meetings, read, cook something healthy, an hour or two of writing. And yet somehow I can shove such a relaxing-looking collection of activities into an inner dialogue: *"OMG! I am never going to manage a walk AND get to yoga AND find time to finish reading all three books I'm in the middle of!! Waa!! Woe is me!!"*

Yes, I realize how idiotic that all sounds, how very First World Problem. Yet when I stop to contemplate the stupidity of getting hyper-agitated over not being able to cram in enough relaxing activities, this just further fuels the agitation and prompts more self-criticism. *I am ungrateful! I am never going to relax! I suck for having accidentally turned into one of those annoying middle-aged ladies I used to hate waiting on in my youth!*

Here on the island is a rare chance to dispense with all that worrying. In fact, so startling is the immediate and notable change in my disposition whenever I am near large bodies of salt water (and especially when I am on islands completely surrounded as opposed to, say, a mere peninsula, or Epsom-enhanced bath) that Warren has asked me many times, and more than half-seriously, why I don't just live at a beach. It's a good question and I'm not entirely sure why, beyond the fact I love Austin and/or maybe Fate is real and has arranged for me to remain landlocked, like some mythical royal human trapped in the body of a warty little toad, until I learn certain life lessons that will free me, which, of course, is totally impossible as these lessons are beyond the grasp of mere mortals.

Besides the Van Gogh painting, this room reminds me of another room, one that exists in my mind only, derived from a time in my life when I wolfed down Hemingway novels in part because I sort of loved them, in part because I think I thought I was supposed to love them, and— at least once— because I was clinging desperately to an unrequited crush on a guy who recommended *Islands in the Stream*.

The Hemingway room of my imagination is less about physical space and objects, and more about a narrative scene in which I have fallen sick, but not *too* sick. Just some vague, extremely minor discomfort that involves exhaustion and requires total quiet and prolonged rest to promote full recovery. As a result, I have been taken to a crisp, white hospital on the edge of the Mediterranean Sea to recuperate as long as necessary. I have been placed in a private room with whitewashed walls. The temperature in this room is perfect— no artificial heating or cooling needed. The windows are open, their frothy, foamy curtains billowing slightly in a very gentle breeze. There are no mosquitoes. The saltiness of the sea fills my nose.

In this room, I sleep more deeply than I have ever slept since the womb. And every few hours a stunning nurse with perky breasts and a dazzling smile and a little white cap with a red cross stamped on the front comes in and feeds me just the right amount of delicious food, which I am able to digest easily. At which point, I fall asleep again. There are no busy charts, no poorly mannered doctors, no scary long-term fallout, no hourly poking and prodding to check my vitals. I am here. I am resting. The world is right.

Walking into my room at the Monhegan House, I am in *L'hôpital de Hemingway*, only it's better than that. Because there is not even a slight hint of illness. Yes, yes, I'm past exhaustion now. And I know if I lie down "for just a minute," I will fall into such a thorough sleep there will be no hope of making it to the dining room for our imminent dinner reservation. Warren, however, has no such concerns. He sprawls out across the blank canvas of our queen-sized Magic Carpet of Sleep and dozes off.

I head off for the shower down the hall— yet another feature I love about this place is the shared commodes, showers and bath, situated behind a row of doors in a hallway. A little indicator on each door lets you know if the toilet/shower/bath is vacant (green) or in use (red). The whole setup—not knowing exactly what is happening behind any given door at any given moment— reminds me of Let's Make a Deal.

If I were to make a list of *The Top Five Consolations for Having Your Travel Plans Totally Fucked Up Thanks to All Flights Being Cancelled in Newark*, surely the delayed reward of a much-longed-for hot shower would hover near the top. Here, in the little shower closet with the cold air sneaking in the cracked open window, competing with the rising steam, I find myself in the state of hyperbole that informs all travel, good and bad. Being on the road makes the bad worse and the good so much better. Here, in this moment, I am convinced that this is the absolute best shower I have had in my entire life, bar none. I linger, I luxuriate, I stop short of letting out an audible, melodramatic sigh, but only because Warren is out of earshot and I'm pretty sure there is no one crapping in the next stall over to witness my joy.

Post shower, noting that Warren is continuing to snore, and seeing we have a few more minutes before dinner, I do what I should not, tug the laptop from its case, hop online to see what mountain of email has built itself in my thirty hours away from the inbox.

Surely there are experts who would argue I am just rationalizing, giving into my compulsion to hit the send/receive button, a sad victim of my OCD tendencies. I would argue back that if they could feel for a half-second the anxiety that riddles me at every turn, and if they could know how far up this anxiety would ratchet should I forego email for an entire week only to return to 500 waiting messages (this really happened the one and only time I did that experiment, when I went on a meditation retreat), they would encourage me to keep right at what I am doing now: *damage control*. I whiz through, ruthlessly discarding without replying to notes the way I would not do in my home office, where I would convince myself that any note short of spam deserves at least some reply. That is my compromise then— not avoiding the mail entirely, but trying to teach myself that the only way to generate less email is to quit with the responding on time, to quit with responding at all if I can get away with that.

And of course, no surprise here, as Warren rolls to his side and dips a little deeper into his nap, I fall a little further down the rabbit hold of virtual correspondence than is acceptable on vacation. Thank goodness for reservations. We wait until the last possible moment, and then a few moments more, and then I hurry Warren to the surface and shut the computer, and we tumble down the stairs, precisely fifteen seconds between our room and the dining room. Technically, we're a little late, but then, we're on Island Time now, so in that sense, we are right on time.

CHAPTER ELEVEN

The feast that awaits us involves far more than food. Once again, we have stepped into a scene, a play, a movie, a novel. Like the bedrooms, the dining room is simple and clean— sturdy, utilitarian tables and utensils, a few paintings on the wall. Otherwise, the space is a *tabula rasa* upon which we can project our own feelings and memories, or choose to leave blank and, taking a cue from the stripped down beauty of it, surrender. As if my ever-racing mind would ever allow this.

Maybe it's a sad thing that, despite more than a decade of meditation practice and a reading list that always includes at least a couple of Buddhist tomes, my mind is never truly going to settle. But I am comforted by relativity, and so here, in this space, I am feeling far calmer and slower than when I am back at home, flitting from one duty to the next.

Angie comes out to greet us and describe the dinner specials. If she herself were a dinner special, she'd be hard to describe, a concoction deceptively simple and straightforward at first glance, but, upon scrutiny, revealed as a complicated flavor combo, one with tart overtones and subtle undertones that do not reveal themselves all at once. She is both personable and distant— pulling us in with her charm yet giving an unspoken but very clear signal that we are different— she is staff, we are guests.

Angie is also extremely efficient and no-nonsense, organized and on top of things despite giving off an air of being laidback and *laissez faire*. She can be engaged in conversation with you one minute, but then, psychically sensing when it's time for her to disappear back into the kitchen, she has the ability to cut you off, pleasantly, just like that. If she could bottle and sell this skill she could make a fortune off of people like me, those of us who've spent a lifetime trying to figure out first what boundaries are and then how to establish and maintain them.

I order butternut squash soup with maple syrup and a salad. Warren orders pork chops. Angie nods, smiles, and disappears. Exhaustion, calm, and excitement all jockey with equal vigor for position in my heart, as if Holden had sneaked up behind me when I wasn't looking and given me three shots in the ass— one tryptophan, one Valium, one adrenaline.

Outside, it is raining and the grass is so green it hurts my eyes. Back in Austin everything has been parched brown for months. What lies beyond the window feels like a trick, an optical illusion. Nothing has ever been so green before.

Just as my hot shower became "the best shower ever taken," and the grass is the "greenest ever grown," our food arrives and fast becomes "the best dinner ever served." I am feeling weepy, a combination of the sleepiness and having every one of my senses assaulted in just the right way— the rich, slightly sweet aroma of the soup, the vivid green of the grass, the sound of the rain and Angie's deep laughter, this solid spoon in my hand delivering smooth thick soup to my tongue. We finish off with three mini-desserts: pumpkin cheesecake, blueberry cobbler, and something chocolate and silky, all served in adorable tiny dishes. Sensual saturation attained, we stumble back up Alcott's staircase and into Hemingway's hospital room and into a deep, deep sleep. It's not even 9 pm.

Forget about sleeping per chance to dream and sign me up for sleep of the dead. After all that driving, those useless McDonald's parking lot catnaps, I am here, cupped in the hands of a benevolent god that places me into a temporary state in which dreams are banished, Warren's snoring is on mute, there is miraculously no fight over the covers or mattress space, and my only job is to conk out and stay conked out for hours and hours of delicious slumber.

We both wake before 5 am, pretty much unheard of in my real life. Though it is still dark, I feel utterly refreshed, solidly rested, and pleasantly cool to the core— chilly even— as I burrow beneath the comforter and allow myself to surface slowly. On the way up, I remember something Holden told us when we checked in. Today is Trap Day, the first day of lobster season, and the lobstermen will be heading out before sunrise to drop thousands of traps. I'd never even heard of Trap Day before, I don't eat lobster, and still I'm as excited as if this is Mardi Gras and I've been designated to play the role of a baby in a King Cake in the school play. Warren is excited, too. This is a chance for him to whip out his eighty-million-dollar camera and shoot something other than me knitting on the ferry, knitting in the lobby, knitting in front of the Monhegan House sign.

We bundle up to steel ourselves for the cold and rain. Warren pulls on his moose hat, one in a series of silly knitted caps I've made at his request over the years. This is a running joke between us that started shortly after we met, when he asked me to knit him some handcuffs, which I did. I then made him a hat with a menorah sticking out of the top for Hanukkah, a hat in the colors of the French flag for our trip to Paris, a gnome hat (with a white beard attached) for a trip he took around the country posing in front of famous landmarks like Mount Rushmore and in the midst of unsuspecting wedding parties, and a bright orange cap topped with a knitted Fanta bottle for a costume known as Fanta Claus.

Warren loves these efforts and marches around bragging about my knitting with the sort of pride more associated with a new father announcing the birth of a child. He doesn't even care how well they turn out, and since I knit them on the fly with no patterns, let's just say results have been uneven at best. Case in point: the moose hat counts as both one of my greatest successes and failures. I was pleased with the ad hoc antlers when they were in progress, but then a little let down to see how they drooped, unable to come up with some knitting version of Viagra to get them to shift from flaccid to erect. In the hat, Warren looks more like a puppy with misshapen ears than a moose, which will generate many confused looks and curious questions once we make our way to the dock.

From Monhegan House front porch to wharf, it can't be more than five blocks as the crow flies. But the fog is thick and a lack of streetlights further hinders our journey as we pick our way carefully and very slowly down the winding path. Again all of my senses are fully engaged: the sounds of excited hollering among the lobstermen and women, the rain and mist on my face, the wet salt in my nostrils, the stacks and stacks of lobster traps— each embellished with a fluorescent buoy painted in a particular pattern to establish its ownership, like metal cattle branded by ocean cowboys.

A small crowd of observers gathers, some momentarily distracted by Warren's odd hat, most focused on the Trap Day trappings. I wish for a coffee and want to cheer when it dawns on me that, of course, the little dock shop is open early on this important day. Not only is steamy coffee ready, but they've got fresh, hot scones, too, scones embedded with melty dark chocolate chips, dusted with cinnamon, and peppered with cayenne powder.

As we sit and unsuccessfully try to slowly savor and not devour the scones, a blockbuster movie trailer unfolds before our very eyes. The young woman working the counter, a stunning beauty of perhaps twenty-two, blushes slightly when a lobsterman, perhaps a few years older than her, comes in to say hello and caffeinate. She is fresh-scrubbed, her blonde tresses pulled into a ponytail, revealing an eager, flawless face. He says something softly to her, indiscernible to us. She looks down for a moment, shy. An incredible buzz invades the room, one absent before he entered the scene.

In the instant that he smiles and she glances away (her rosy cheeks growing rosier) the plot unfolds and again my imagination roars awake. *Have they kissed yet? If not, will they? Does she already have a boyfriend? Does he have a girlfriend? Will they find true love? Is she just summer help? Will her love for him keep her here on the island forever and ever? Will they have babies? Will she learn to go out on Trap Day? Will they stay in love forever? Will they grow to resent each other? Will they continue serving these fucking amazing scones? Please God, say yes!!*

Then the lobsterman steps out to do his duties on the water, and we step outside too, and Warren disappears, off to shoot and shoot and shoot and shoot and shoot— hundreds of pictures of thousands of traps from countless angles. I stake out a spot and watch and listen, my attention pulled in a few different directions.

There is the big picture— all of those traps transforming dock into labyrinth, rows and rows of stacks and stacks that you could, if it didn't mean being in the way of the workers, slip along and behind, imagining yourself to be a little child pretending to be an explorer in a forest of metal dotted with the psychedelic contrast of the buoys. Even in the pre-dawn darkness and thick fog, the colors leap out, as does the bright yellow of the head-to-toe rain suits worn by the lobstermen and lobsterwomen and at least one little lobsterchild, done up like a miniature sales rep for Gorton's of Gloucester.

The atmosphere is a mix of seriousness— hauling the traps onto the boats is hard work in a tight space— and festive. Though there aren't nearly as many tourists here on the first day of October, there are still enough of us and we are excited witnesses to the bustle. Some have volunteered to help, as have seasonal residents like Holden. This is certainly an all-hands-on-deck affair and everyone has a job, even if that job is to stay out of the way and not ask too many questions.

I spot Birdman and his girlfriend. The sky lightens as we talk—thanks to the fog there will be no official sunrise. The first boat, weighed down with traps, sets out and everyone is laughing and cheering and waving. Warren is gone long enough that I begin to wonder if he's wandered back up to bed and I think about how I, with my constant low-level anxiety and herding instincts, always feel a need to keep track of all pack members at any given moment. Warren does not share this need, is relaxed enough to just know that sooner or later, especially on a tiny island, we're bound to catch up with each other sooner or later. Finally I spot him, snapping away happily with his camera, his droopy moose-puppy antlers looking utterly ridiculous.

As the dock empties of traps and more boats set off, we reunite and head back up to the house. It's not even 8 am yet and we've been up for hours. We wander into the dining room and settle in for breakfast, never mind that I'm still digesting the scones. The food here is so exquisite, I don't want to miss a meal. At the table next to us sits a family of four, a young couple and two very young kids. Angie is our server and theirs, and I am delighted to have a ringside seat where I can observe her no-nonsense style.

While she's off in the kitchen putting in an order, I eavesdrop on the family. The young parents are painstakingly offering the kids myriad choices, ticking off menu items, over-explaining everything, and the kids, in response, are within an inch of actually running the show, or maybe they are running the show. Angie approaches them, asks what they'd like to order, and upon hearing the request of one child, says frankly and without apology, her voice on the edge of a bark, "Nope. Don't have that. Pick something else."

I hear a bigger message in her words: *Look kids, you're not going to get everything in your life, and really that's no big whoop, just figure out something else and let's get on with it.* And perhaps to the astonishment of their parents— likely waiting for a tantrum to ensue— the kids, maybe shocked into compliance or maybe just getting her message and appreciating the directness, readily make another choice.

After they leave, after Warren and I have stopped just short of licking our breakfast plates clean, Angie comes by to offer one more coffee refill. I tell her how much I enjoyed watching her be so straightforward with the kids, and she takes a moment to talk about the wonders of dealing with diners, day in and day out, again transporting me back to my own days as a waiter.

She retrieves a menu, opens it, and points to the section listing sides. "See that?" she says, her finger landing on *Fresh Fruit*. "Last year, it used to say *Fruit Cup* there. And now it clearly says *Fresh Fruit*. But I've had customers come back, point right at the words *Fresh Fruit* and say, 'I'll have the *Fruit Cup*,' as if they can magically turn it back into what it was, what they want it to be, just by saying it."

I laugh and not just at the idiocy of other people. I laugh because in my own fashion, I am at times guilty of similar behavior. I like to think I try to keep this sense of entitlement in check, and that I am an unfussy customer, flexible and willing to go along. But even if I have trained myself (most of the time) to not ask for special treatment, I don't think I'll ever stop secretly hoping special treatment awaits me.

Happily weighed down with our breakfasts, we climb the stairs back to our room. My job, and it's a really tough one for me, is to keep my head from thinking about the clock, about how few our hours are on the island, and to just try hard to follow the day. I plop down on the big, inviting Hemingway Hospital bed and lean back against a Rubenesque pillow and open up the Buddhist nun's memoir.

I love this book. I love entertaining the fantasy of becoming a Buddhist nun. This daydream is less rooted in faith than the promise of massive amounts of solitude, a ready excuse to not be on the computer, an opportunity to simplify. Daydream melts into sleepiness, eyes now heavy as my stomach. I drift far away, fall deep, deep into it. Naps are such a rarity— I have spent decades following in the footsteps of my hero grandmother, Murphy Mom-Mom, who loved to say, "I'll sleep when I'm dead." Busy is in my blood. Convincing myself now to surrender to slumber is a true feat. Warren, the Nap King, falls asleep beside me, that cool damp air wandering in through the window still an exotic sensation, a sleeping potion.

When we resurface, to my amazement it still isn't noon yet. Not noon? I've already witnessed Trap Day, downed two scones, slurped a half-gallon of coffee, wolfed a full breakfast, engaged in a funny conversation with Angie *and* indulged in a rare nap and it's still morning? *I need to live here* scrolls across the inner LED screen of my mind. Now it's time to get up and to show Warren yet another reason I don't ever want to stop coming here: the hiking trails.

Around behind the Monhegan House is a little take-out place called the Novelty. Sue— not Holden's wife, another Sue— runs the joint. She is weathered but not craggy, direct but not unfriendly. Her wavy wiry gray hair is cropped around her deeply tanned face. The dishes she serves combine elements of comfort food with gourmet surprise. Before Warren and I decide which hike to take, we stop in and contemplate available snacks for our journey. I select a pumpkin whoopie pie, though the decision is not without some hemming and hawing and a touch of agony. Because Sue has also made the more traditional chocolate whoopie pies, creating a real dilemma.

Whoopie pies. Before my first trip to Maine, I had never heard of these delicacies. Now I know they have a history and are even the center of a dispute. Pennsylvania and Maine both claim rights to their origin. The former says the whole thing started with the Amish. The latter, perhaps hoping to end the argument, named the Whoopie Pie the Official State Snack. Frankly, I don't give a damn where they came from, I just know that when I die and am buried, I'd like my headstone carved to resemble one and to feature just one word: Whoopie!

Think of a mutant Oreo, much larger than the original, and made from Devil's Food cake filled with a massive dollop of cream. In my youth, I had a love affair with Drake's Devil Dogs, a distant cousin of the whoopie pie—oblong in shape, the cake portion of this confection far more dry and crumbly than the masterpieces Sue turns out. Once I had my first Sue-baked whoopie pie, though, there was no turning back. I immediately had my second and my third. As the years rolled on and I came to know I would be back again, I learned to pace myself a little better, which is why this year I force myself to choose between pumpkin and chocolate rather than give in and buy both.

Oh Whoopie Pie! You delectable, irresistible thing, you. Get in my mouth! I let Warren have a bite or two, then polish off the rest of this fist-sized treat myself. Probably not the more advisable nourishment to fuel an hours-long trek through the forest and along cliffs, but at least for the first half-hour I will be carried along by a magnificent rush of refined sugar blasting through my veins.

CHAPTER TWELVE

In a world where, anymore, even small children can figure out how to click on a map app and get detailed GPS assistance and see satellite views of their houses, the paper map offered to island visitors is quaint to say the least. Sketched on a single sheet of paper, it more resembles a pretend map used in a make-believe game of Find the Buried Treasure. Solid lines mark easy trails, mostly flat, that cut across forest floors. Dotted lines mark slightly more challenging trails, the promise of loose rocks along the way, and an occasional incline. Paths indicated by diamonds count as the genuinely tricky areas, all of which lie along the island's coast and most of which place hikers atop towering cliffs.

Advisories to pay attention, use caution, and not tread into areas clearly marked dangerous are not to be taken lightly. Just a month before our trip, an tourist was grabbed by a wave and killed in an instant, his companions stuck for hours on a tiny rock shelf, horrified, unable to render assistance or escape themselves to call for help. And yet, even with such horror stories to serve as cautionary tales, I can attest from personal experience that the rugged beauty is so alluring, so hypnotizing, that you can wander, quite accidentally, into a No Go Zone, as sunlight diamonds dancing across the Atlantic pull you forward before you even realize you've gone too far.

On our trip to Hawaii, Warren and I spent one day hiking where we thought we understood the map but then, about six hours past the time we should have been finished, still wandering around a massive field of lava, we had to admit we were lost. Not Big Lost, as in the choppers would have to come looking. But lost enough to know that if we didn't get our bearings soon enough, we might be in for a chilly night out in the elements.

Though Monhegan is a speck by comparison to the Big Island, this, too, is a place where you can get disoriented, with trail markers often so tiny it's hard not to think the locals did this purposefully, not so much out of mean spiritedness but as some kind of reminder that outsiders will always be just that. My lack of sense of direction has an upside to it here— because no trail ever reaches the point of feeling fully familiar to me, even when I am on a hike I've taken numerous times before, the path feels brand new to me.

At the same time, islands offer me some comfort in the face of my woeful directional challenges— if I get really, truly lost then I can keep walking and walking and I will, eventually, reach a cliff, and then I can walk the perimeter until I find civilization. A rather ridiculous solution, but if you are someone who understands the panic that is the constant companion of those of us with zero sense of direction, you'll know the relief that even a clearly time-consuming emergency plan can bring.

We head first up toward the lighthouse, passing the scattering of little shops until the "downtown district" is behind us. This takes about two minutes. There are houses along the way, and each of these invites me to make up stories about the families that first stayed in them, and to wonder how in the hell they got all that lumber out to the island in the first place, and to further ponder how in the hell electricity works here, and to wonder what it must've been like before electricity, back when candles provided the only light, wood the only warmth.

The lighthouse museum is closed, but we stop to take some pictures and sit on the bench out front and look down on the little bit of trail we've covered, the old cemetery, and out across the ocean. I am happy, humming along with my sugar buzz, giddy at showing Warren yet another spot I love here. It's chilly and damp and I'm wearing a scarf and thinking about how it is 110 degrees back in Austin.

Then off we go to Cathedral Woods. Trees everywhere, some standing tall and mighty, others fallen and exposing mammoth root clumps in various stages of decay. Mossy, moist, verdant, magical— pick your *Lord of the Rings* adjective and apply it liberally here. We will come across a few other hikers along the way, but mostly we get the place to ourselves, this being the off-season. Every mushroom, every flower, every birdsong, every raindrop— nothing I've not seen or heard or smelled before and yet as fresh and unknown as if I've just landed on another planet, this thanks in large part to having just spent the past several months in my parched and brittle home state.

We take our time. We stop to investigate the Fairy Houses that dot the forest floor, tiny edifices built from objects of nature and left behind by sly architects for observant passersby to discover. Some of these miniature structures are lean-tos, about to fall over, barely embellished at all. Others resemble swank Fairy Condos, chockfull of amenities— paved path of pebbles leading to a front door fashioned from bark, a carport, mossy chandeliers, mini-pinecone staircases, roofs thatched in long, dried pine needles. There is waterfront property, too, Fairy Houses erected along little streams. All of these structures are teeny-tiny, studded with itty-bitty snail shells, sea glass, soft moss and the occasional red-mottled or yellowing leaf.

Leaves. You never know for sure when the leaves will turn. They have minds of their own. My first trip to Maine in 2008 they were barely turning when I arrived and by the time I was preparing to depart just a week later, the state was ablaze in a riot of rich hues. On this trip things are mostly still green, but green remains such an exotic color to us, given the desert conditions back in Texas, that we still experience the thrilling effect of nature changing her wardrobe. We also know that, given our plans to spend several more days on the mainland once we leave the island, we might just yet encounter a stretching roadside canopy of crimson and tumeric and tangerine.

Heading out of Cathedral Woods it doesn't take ten minutes for us to unintentionally step onto a different path than the one we had decided on. I had suggested we head to Pebble Beach, which I love because the name is ironic and the view is— pardon the cliché but it is apt— breathtaking. Massive boulders that have been endlessly tumbled by the sea smooth over, become God's bowling balls, and cover this crescent stretch. Pebbles? Hardly.

Somehow, though, we wind up reaching the coast some distance from our intended destination. Stubborn me— I remain determined to reach my original goal. This means navigation that will now require tackling some difficult patches made more daunting still courtesy of the rain-slick, slippery slopes.

While I love hiking, certain moments on certain hikes have caused that love to be lost, at least temporarily. The most common trigger for such rapid loss of affection occurs when a certain elevation is reached and looking down causes my healthy fear of heights to escalate into an unhealthy acrophobia that can trigger panic attacks. Onset is sudden and crippling, prompting a sneakers-tumbling-in-dryer sensation in my stomach, shortness of breath, and paralysis of rational thinking, which yes, sounds a lot like the first stages of romantic love, but, I assure you, is far less joyful. (Not limited to outdoor nature climbs, this phobia occurs in human-made structures, too, such as when I was cajoled into ascending and/or descending the staircases inside the Lewis and Clark Tower in Oregon, the Texas State Capitol, and the Eiffel Tower.)

The cliffs on Monhegan Island feel mostly manageable, though there are spots that make me wonder if this island has in mind to chew me up and spit me out. But these spots are scattered at great intervals, with lulling easy paths in between providing ample opportunities to collect myself and steady my breathing. And even along the more dangerous spots there is almost always a tree or shrub to grab onto when foot hits loose root or hydroplanes across slick rock. So I am, mostly, okay with this trek, difficult enough to make me feel like I'm accomplishing something, but not so difficult as to drive me into hyperventilation.

Hiking is something Warren and I should do every day. On the trail together we sing, we laugh, we joke. *Hi-ho, hi-ho, it's off to Pebble Beach we go.* Back when I was still a big boozehound, I used to sit on the porch nearly every night and throw back a six-pack, sometimes with friends, sometimes alone. Looking back, I think my favorite part of this ritual came somewhere in between beer three and beer four.

The sensation lasted only for a fleeting window of about twenty minutes, but during this time I was— or perceived myself to be— relaxed. Happy. Not worried. Able to sit still. All things that eluded me during the rest of the day. Ultimately the hangovers and bad feelings weren't worth it, but I remember that fleeting good feeling. This is how a long hike is for me. When I am hiking, I am free, floating, not thinking about appointments or deadlines beckoning. This is the ultimate getting-away-with-it feeling.

Inside my daypack, I carry too many energy bars (just in case we do manage to miraculously get truly lost and have to sleep in the woods overnight), my headlamp (handy not just for hiking in the dark, but also for seeing my knitting in the dim evening light of the Monhegan House parlor), my knitting (natch) and, *what's this here?* I cannot believe it when I see it. My own business card which, when flipped over, reveals the name and address of my friend Isabel, which she herself scrawled there, in her own hand.

Finding this card in my fanny pack both surprises me and doesn't. The small surprise comes from thinking that I'd actually left this card tucked into the little outer plastic sleeve on the back of my suitcase, designated for an identification card. I do not remember moving it from there to here. The non-surprise is this: Considering how Isabel was in life, seeming to show up just when I needed her, it makes easy sense that here she is now. Looking at her name, I am delighted and pleasantly spooked. My mind floats back to our limited but precious moments together.

I met Isabel on the island, and one of my best adventures here was thanks to her. All told we probably only spent maybe four or five hours of face-to-face time together, these spread across a couple of trips. But she wrapped deep roots and abundant life around my heart swiftly, the way a sweet potato in a jar of water fills up a kitchen with cheery green leaves in no time. She died suddenly, a couple of months after the last time I'd seen her, and I had not been able to attend her memorial, held in the little chapel on the island. Now, her name surfacing in this funny way, I have an unexpected but most welcome chance to take her along on a final hike with me.

I run through the short but amazing Story of Us as I chug through the glorious foliage. Isabel and I met in 2009 when she and her husband, Joe were staying at the Monhegan House the same time as the knitting group. They'd spent summers on Monhegan for many decades, had known Holden's family forever. She was a knitter, too, and upon discovering this, I eagerly invited her to sit in on an evening fireside knit with us. She was happy to join in, bringing along a sweater she'd been knitting for Joe.

Isabel's magic was instantly palpable, and she was one of those people that others are irresistibly drawn to and, literally, wished to sit nearer to. She had a built-in irony in that every story she told was fascinating, and yet she seemed to prefer to listen. This caused a most pleasant conflict in me, a no-lose scenario in which I was either hearing amazing tales of her childhood or unburdening my heart with full cathartic abandon, like I had stepped straight out of Dostoevsky novel.

That first night knitting she laughed with us and listened and her aura gave off a glow at least as warm as the fire. Her hair— gray and soft and wild— suggested she was in her seventies, as did her beautifully aged skin. But her attitude and her energy weighed in somewhere between utterly youthful and eternally ageless. Was she even real? She was ethereal and fully grounded simultaneously. Someone mentioned to her that I had a new book out, and look, here was a copy, and Isabel held it in her hands like she was cradling a first grandchild, and *oohed* and *ahhed* over it, prompting in me a mortified-with-joy embarrassment that made me feel like a beautiful child.

It so happened that a day or two after I met Isabel, I managed a rather difficult feat. Though I was on the island, far away from Warren, and though connectivity was shoddy, I instigated and then escalated an argument, based on what could and should have remained a little drama, something to be swatted away like a gnat. Instead, a molehill became a volcano as I spewed and sputtered and rumbled my way into a rage, calling Warren repeatedly, cursing Skype every time the call dropped, calling again, whipping myself into a most unreasonable state.

I spotted Isabel in the dining room, breakfasting alone the morning after the worst of my battle with Warren. She seemed so peaceful sitting there that, though I longed to join her, I thought it better for me to give her space. I did stop by her table as I was leaving, and she smiled radiantly and invited me to sit with her. I accepted, eagerly, and this became a game-changing occasion in life for me, one of those wildly rare *When the student is ready, the teacher will appear* moments. Though in this case "ready" did not mean "visibly calm and clearly open to wisdom thanks to much preparation and contemplation." Instead, it meant I was ready for the top of my head to blow off with fury, and Isabel sensed this, I think, easily saw through the cheery façade I tried to present as I sat down.

We began our talk with me coaxing from her some of her story, happy to turn the tables on her after she'd been such a good listener the night before. English by birth, she'd grown up in China, her family held in an interment camp during World War II, when she was a small child. She'd lived in the States with Joe for a very long time now, and her English accent was faint, reshaped a bit by the peculiarities of New England vowels. Isabel's tales were dramatically compelling, though she chose to deliver them calmly, tales of imprisonment spoken matter-of-factly.

I learned she was a writer, too, and was working on a biography of Mary Baker Eddy, founder of the Church of Christ, Scientist. I told her I'd written for the *Christian Science Monitor* and she said she had, too. Writing for that institution's paper hardly made me an expert on the religion— the *CSM*'s content is secular, highly regarded, and award-winning journalism. But, I had a vague notion that the church eschews medical intervention. This thought popped into my head then, followed immediately by another— Isabel must be a healer of some sort. I broached the topic. She confirmed my hunch. I was too shy to press her for more information. Did she tell me she helped prepare people for death or am I imagining this only in the wake of her own?

Doesn't matter. Point is, I knew then that she was a healer— knew it yes, because of a thing or two she mentioned, but also *knew it*, inside of me, because of what I felt sitting there in her presence. Moments before, I'd been eating my breakfast, in a rage at Warren, being devoured alive by my anger. Now calm enveloped me, almost against my will, as I sat listening to Isabel's soft, deep, touch-of-England voice.

We wrapped up our conversation with an invitation extended and accepted. Isabel suggested we take in the sunrise together the next morning at Burnt Head, the eastern edge of the island, a brisk fifteen-minute hike from Monhegan House. I told her I'd meet her there.

Next morning, pre-dawn, I bundled up and headed down the path, hustling, afraid that I'd get there too late. Funny, I can't even remember now if there was a crisp sunrise, though I'm pretty sure the clouds obscured the lifting orange disc from clear view. But there is a sight I won't ever forget. As I came through the brush leading to the rocks upon which I saw Isabel already situated—who knows how early she'd gotten up— I was torn between wanting to remain silent, so as not to disturb her, and wanting to make a gentle noise, so as not to startle her.

Once she spotted me, she gestured me over and I took my place beside her. And then, less than twenty-four hours after she'd given me one life-changing moment, she gave me another. Reaching into her pocket, she extracted a small object, something silver and round. I confess that when I first spotted the thing, I thought, "Now why would Isabel have a rape whistle out here?"

She solved the mystery for me, swinging apart on a little hinge the two main components of the object. "A friend gave this to me," she said. "It's a jeweler's loupe."

Isabel then explained the power of the loupe to me. "Come over here," she said, as we were walking together back to Monhegan House. She bent over a plant, held her loupe up close to its tiny flower, leaned in for a good look, and proclaimed, *"MAGNIFICENT!"*

She handed the loupe to me. I bent down, squinted my eye as I held up the lens. I looked and saw a full universe of details unseeable to my naked eye. The view truly was magnificent.

Upon my return to Texas, it took a while for things to settle between Warren and me. We'd done significant damage, both of us, to each other and our relationship, with that long distance argument. But he went a long way toward soothing me when one day he handed me my own jeweler's loupe, knowing how much I had enjoyed that hike with Isabel, and how much she had helped me. *Magnificent!* became part of our private lexicon, a reminder to ourselves to remember to appreciate the great beauty in small things. The loupe came with us on day trips, and we took turns holding it close to all manner of objects, natural and human-made: a cotton boll, a dead beetle, a gadget. "Magnificent!" we would proclaim. *"Magnificent!"*

I kept the loupe draped over my rearview mirror, a daily reminder of Isabel. I sent her a copy of my quilting book, the one she'd admired in the parlor, and included a card thanking her for the gift of her presence, vaguely explaining that when she'd sat with me that morning in the dining room I had been suffering and her words had been so healing. Thus began our pen pal relationship, a snail mail/e-mail hybrid, exchanging books, pictures, cards, copies of the *Christian Science Monitor*, updates and good cheer.

The next year, 2010, I emailed her a month or so before the knitting retreat to let her know my dates on the island. She said she might not be able to make it then, that she was expecting out-of-town guests. But the guests changed their dates allowing Isabel and Joe to come to the island, which at the time seemed like just a bit of good luck, but ultimately proved to be an overwhelmingly large gift of Fate.

I was so eager to see Isabel, to hug her, to hear her voice. I'd brought along a gift for her, a funny children's book called *Who*

Needs Donuts? that is a lovely little tale about love. Better still, it is packed with hyper-detailed illustrations, images so tiny that *Where's Waldo?* seems broad stroke by comparison. The book is perfect fodder for loupe viewing, and I was excited to point out spots I wanted Isabel to closely scrutinize with her little magnifying glass.

I can see her so clearly, in her own Hemingway Hospital Room down the hall from mine at Monhegan House. I can see her cheerful smile and hear her playfully calling Joe "Giuseppe," like they'd just met, and were still teenagers trying out pet names on one another.

The next day Isabel and I went down to a little shack by the inlet that sells chowder and lobster. She told me about a dish she liked, salmon and hash potatoes, and we each ordered up a plate. We drank the dirty-colored water and waited for our salty, tasty entrees, served on paper plates that we scraped clean, leaving greasy Rorsarch spots behind. The seagulls circled overhead as we caught each other up on our lives. We spent a bit more time together before she and Joe left.

Two months later, she was dead. Holden sent me a terse email with word that she was gone, no details. He sent another months later, to let me know of the island memorial.

When I first checked in with Warren on this trip, I asked Holden for more information about Isabel's death. She'd been swimming in a pool when something went wrong— a stroke maybe. Revived by EMS workers, she then lingered a few days before dying. Her service on the island, the one I'd had to miss, commenced just before sunrise, when all gathered hiked out to Burnt Head, the beautiful place she'd loved and visited for forty years, the place where she introduced me to the loupe and the magnificence it revealed.

Finding her card in my goofy fanny pack now, on this hike with Warren, I smile, hold it up for him to see, and announce,

"Look, Isabel is with us!" We proceed to proclaim the magnificence of everything around us, both in her honor and also because everything really is magnificent.

That night, after our wonderfully achingly long hike, we wind up back at the Novelty. Sue comes out from behind the counter and approaches our table. "You were friends with Isabel, weren't you?" she asks, and I am honored to be remembered like this— a friend of Isabel.

"Yes," I say. "And you'll never guess what happened today!" I reach into my pack to pull out the card on which Isabel had written her name, to show Sue proof of my story, to proudly clutch at this little souvenir of our friendship, as if owning it makes me some sort of Super Special Friend of Isabel. But the card is gone. Vanished completely.

It's as if Isabel had taken that last hike with me, offered some reassurance from whatever beyond she now occupies, and then, job finished, she just disappeared.

CHAPTER THIRTEEN

We wind up in bed by 7 pm that night, worn out from the excitement of pre-dawn Trap Day, the much longer than expected hike, and residual lagging from our days-before all-night road trip. The weather, still cold and wet, and October's early evening darkness lend themselves well to this decision to retire at a bedtime more suited to toddlers and octogenarians.

I struggle to keep my eyes open, determined that I will, before this trip is over, finish the slim volume I'm reading about the young Buddhist nun. Actually, as ever, I've brought along several books, thinking I'll tackle at least two, preferably more. Now it's looking like I'd be lucky to read fifty pages total. But another bright side of vacation is that I am, if only slightly, better able to cut myself a little slack when I don't manage to hit certain goals such as *Read Ten Books in a Week*.

Exhaustion, particularly the sort brought on by rigorous physical exertion, is a wonderful excuse for further surrender. And surrender I do once again, my eyes getting droopier. Warren, rather to my surprise, reaches down for my feet. Foot rubs are by and away my favorite form of intimate contact, and Warren is no slouch in the reflexology department. But he's exhausted, too. So to have him indulge my fetish, sans my requesting it, prompts an intense and instantly noticeable shift in me.

In the moments that he rubs my feet, and then the rest of me, deep massaging every spot until my body is just this side of a joyful coma, I recapture that utterly giddy adolescent "in love" feeling that had long ago left the building for us. This is not to say we stopped loving each other. But time, volatility, and familiarity long ago stripped off the goggles of early infatuation. Most days we are content. Sometimes— though less and less often— one or both of us will start humming the *Let's Break Up* theme song which, the more years we are together, the more it seems like we really need to rewrite the song. Perhaps something like *Let's Break Up for a Half-Hour or So.*

    Rare, though, are the goo-goo moments like the one that has just crept up on us. Warren gets out his iPod and puts one earbud in my ear and the other in his and plays some Rufus Wainwright, just like he did the Christmas Day we were in Paris, buried under the blankets in the apartment borrowed from friends, staving off the bitter cold and that holiday, which I loathe. That was another time I distinctly remember feeling overwhelmed with Warren Love.

    Remember this, I tell myself, snuggled under the comforter, burrowed up against Warren. *Memorize it. Know that it's real. Recall this next time you're fighting and don't forget that this place, this love, is as real as any anger or arguing is. Hold onto it.*

    As if. As if any of us can hold onto any moment or conjure it back up as needed to stave off a brewing storm. At least my note-to-self to memorize the moment does not totally steal from me the moment itself. I am able to sink into the moment as it is happening, to feel that sweeping love, like a lightning bolt, an epiphany, some ghost I waited up all night for.

    The next morning, though we've convinced Holden to let us check out late, there is an early knock on the door. The maid, a young woman from Eastern Europe, wants access to our room. I know this is her last day, that the hotel is closing up for the winter. I protest, but not much. She replies with a hard stare, stereotypical and caricature of her culture. She wins.

    And so, instead of a slow and relaxing exit from our little faux-hospital room, Warren and I hustle to clear out our things. The ferry— we are catching the late one— is hours from arriving. The rain is coming down hard. We move downstairs, eat another hearty breakfast, then sink down into the big leather couch in the parlor by the fireplace.

I gulp down more about the Buddhist nun and take copious notes in my journal. Warren sits nearby, within reach, busy in his own mind. This is a version of perfect for me, reinforcing my fantasy that I could— *really I could, couldn't I?* — give up my busy life back home, move to this place, sit in this spot, read all damn day long, log off, tune in, drop out. Forever.

I know, I know, without my busy life back home to serve as foil, these stolen, fleeting moments of relaxing wouldn't mean as much. But then, I argue with myself, maybe they would. And as I always think whenever I am on an island, *"I have no idea why I don't live on an island. I must move to an island before I die."*

I leave Warren for a brief stretch, walk down the front steps of the Monhegan House, the spot where Isabel and I were last photographed together the year before, and then step ten feet across the dirt path, now muddy, and over to the tiny island church. I'd intended to try to make it to the Blessing of the Animals, held earlier in the morning, but let the weather talk me out of it.

Now, entering the empty chapel and seeing the still remaining efforts of the organizer, I'm kicking myself. Up on the board announcing the day's hymns, instead of words there are tiny paw and hoof prints. And on the arm of each pew are little plastic figurines of animals: zebra, elephant, horse, goat and, up close to the lectern, a dinosaur. A dinosaur! Humor and effort are two of my favorite characteristics in humans. That someone took the time to gussy up the church for a little ceremony on a rainy day to honor animals hits me deep in my gut.

I sit for a while in the back pew, meditating, thinking of Isabel, loving Monhegan Island. Given my disdain for the Catholicism foisted on me as a child, and all those times being forced to go into a church, and all my disgust with the pedophiliac priest scandals and every bit of bullshit to emanate from every pope I've ever heard quoted, you'd think churches might give me the creeps. No. I like the idea of sanctuary. I am awed by the notion of faith. I can separate out my anger at power-hungry assholes that seize on organized religion as a means of controlling others from my respect for those who wish for a quiet place to worship. I won't ever go in for organized religion again myself, but when I am in a church like this, I can feel all the good things that believing brings people.

The last hour or two slips away from us. We wander over to the Black Duck Emporium, a little café and gift shop, dubbed by my knitting retreat fellows as The Mall, the place where we buy still more bags for our projects. Few things make me as happy as a rich hot chocolate at the Black Duck, served in a white mug with red lobster logo on it, overflowing with pure, über fluffy whipped cream. An orange tabby joins us, walking back and forth across the table, swishing her tail around Warren's face. I sit, in anorak and hand-knitted hat and cowl, working on a bright orange honeycomb cable scarf, a royal pain in the ass save for the fact its recipient is a dear friend, making the hard work well worth it. Then back for one last little set-down in the Monhegan House parlor until, too soon, time comes for us to head down to the dock to catch the 4:30 ferry ride back across.

We bid Holden and Sue a farewell, and I promise I'll be back. Then onto the ferry, empty save for crew and four other passengers. The ride is not an easy one and I glance peripherally at the couple across from us, their heads bowed onto the edge of the seats in front of them as they strive to not blow major chunks.

I pride myself in my mostly iron stomach, but the iron gives way to something more like Jell-o as we bounce along, and I tell myself what I always tell myself when on choppy seas or flying through turbulent air: "You've made the decision to be here. You're here. You can't get off now so just shut up and put up." Thankfully, I keep my light breakfast down. Warren, King of the Nap, falls fast asleep like he has just sunk down into the perfectly adjusted Sleep Number mattress, apparently not even slightly affected by the chop.

Then, back to semi-reality. Not total reality, not the rush of my life in Austin, my constant emails. But back to a car, and driving, and having to pay more attention to my surroundings. Before departing Port Clyde, I pop into the general store for some crackers and soda, hoping to settle my stomach, which is still twitching even though we are back on land.

We set the GPS for a little town a few hours to the north, where my friends Vince and Diana live with their kids, Fiona and Peter. Once again observing the glacially slow speed limits along the way, we quite literally wind our way on curvy roads through tiny towns. The rain prevails, as does the chill, offering up additional challenges. Fear of hydroplaning slows me down even more than legally required at particularly hairy curves, and Warren and I proceed to engage in our ongoing, passive-aggressive, climate control dance/argument, each of us adjusting the heater (me up, him down) as surreptitiously as possible, as if the sudden jump or drop in temperature won't be instantly noticed by the other.

Though I've stayed with Diana and Vince before, it's been a couple of years, and that, along with my usual crappy sense of direction and a slightly impaired GPS, find us just lost enough that by the time we do pull into the long drive of their converted 1840s farmhouse, the kids are already in bed. This is a huge disappointment, but when I hear them still awake at the top of the stairs, I ask Diana, who is standing at the kitchen island kneading a bowlful of sourdough, if I might please, please, sneak up for a quick hello. She consents, an affirmative delivered in her fading but still discernable German accent, and I scurry up the stairs.

I love these kids both for the delightful creatures they are, and also for how they represent the kooky, delightful turns life can take. I know them because a full quarter century ago, in the summer of 1987 in Knoxville, Tennessee, I dated their father for roughly forty-five seconds.

Vince and I had been setup by a close mutual friend, the idea being that we'd have a casual date or two before he moved away to West Virginia. Me being me, I'd gotten attached (very), not just thanks to Vince's good looks and beautiful singing, but very much by virtue of the fact that he said he was leaving. Unavailable? Perfect! My kind of guy. It fell to my then twenty-three year old heart to convince him to stay, or at least stay in a relationship.

Vince wasn't going to allow that to happen, though. We spent a few weeks hanging out, him strumming Tom Waits tunes for me on his little screened-in balcony as we created a narrative for Harlan, his "pet" praying mantis that lived on that porch. We got loaded in bars, hit a few parties, and one night, drunk, he drove me out to the country, to a friend's place, and we camped out in an abandoned pigsty, where I awoke in the morning to discover he had headed back to town without me.

Still, my heart pined for him when he moved away, and I made a pilgrimage or two or three to his A-frame in the West Virginia woods. He was having no part of my notion of continuing what had been a poor excuse of a romance to begin with. I think he'd agree with my sense that back then, though he wasn't exactly cruel, he had a hint of a mean streak— not rooted in blatant maliciousness, but more centered on self-concern. But Vince grew into himself, and became a gentle man— albeit a stubborn one—

and eventually husband to a strong, beautiful woman and father to two preternaturally intelligent, curious and compassionate children.

That the two of us, so incredibly different on the surface, would come to stay friends for decades amuses us. Though Vince would laugh in my face at the notion, I sometimes like to chalk up our similarities to astrology. We are just four days apart in age, both goat-headed Capricorns. By my reckoning, our shared trait of supreme stubbornness encompasses deep loyalty and dedication, quite possibly explaining how we held onto the friendship for so long.

Whatever the force that kept us in one another's orbit, I'm grateful for it. I remember once, in the early '90s when I was already in Austin, Vince sent my way a recent ex of his who was traveling through. I forget her name but remember the encounter. She was fascinating, strong, and inspirational. We got along great. But the best proof of his excellent taste in women is Diana, an absolute human dynamo. Before we ever even met in person we became phone friends.

In early 2007, when my last marriage was falling apart, she offered counsel from afar, and her deep empathy soothed me during that tumultuous period of constant headfuck. This conversation led to others, and to the exchange of letters and gifts. In 2008, when I took my second trip to Monhegan Island, afterwards I traveled up to meet her and the kids in person for the first time.

Walking into her house is like stepping back in time. Way back in time. Diana likes to muse that really she should've lived in the 13th century. She and Vince raise, grow and hunt their own food: eggs, veggies, venison and moose meat. They chop wood, keep a fire stoked, eschew TV. Diana home schools the kids, spins wool, and knits sweaters and socks like a madwoman, zipping along on the needles in a manner I won't ever achieve, not now after a dozen years of knitting, not if I knit for another four dozen years.

This lifestyle they've chosen is not without modern conveniences—electricity, email, internet for example. Nor have they chosen it to lord some holier-than-thou shit over urban dwellers and suburban Big Box addicts. This is just The Way It Is for them and that they found each other is a testament to something good. Their kids are two of the most amazing humans I've met.

In 2010, Diana brought Peter and Fiona to Monhegan Island. They drove down to Port Clyde and caught the ferry across, and their genuine enthusiasm for the boat ride thrilled their fellow passengers. Their excitement at being on the island was equally infectious. The fact that Holden only had a tiny, slant-ceilinged fourth-floor room with just a single bed did not dent their joy—they set up pallets on the floor. And when these two children sat down in the parlor to knit alongside their mother, my knitting group did a collective swoon. *They can knit!*

The trio barely stayed 24 hours, but we more than made the most of our little window of time. The hike we took included some strenuous turns, and without hesitation whenever I stumbled or reached what felt like an impasse, little Peter was right beside me, reaching out for my hand, coaxing me along. This, I later joked, he must've gotten from his mother, because I could still remember a time, twenty years before, when on a visit to see his dad I'd requested a "good hike," and only after I completed it without collapsing did Vince admit that he'd purposefully chosen a trek designed to push me beyond my limits, and that to tell the truth he was pretty surprised I made it the whole way.

That was always Vince's sense of humor. Leave me in a pigsty, select a hell hike, leave a realistic looking rubber snake in the guest room bed for me to discover in the dark. Laconic much of the time (leaving my imagination to fill in all that blank, quiet air with endless narratives about *what he must be thinking*), his quietness and prank-playing found an excellent counterbalance in Diana's nurturing ways, her innate compassion, her love of conversation.

The kids crawled all over the orange rusted skeleton of an old shipwreck, regaled me with tales of more difficult hikes they'd taken, and taught me the joys of searching for sea glass tumbled and smoothed and polished in the surf. I was sorry to see them go the next day, and eager for our next encounter.

Now here we are a year later, and after my quick greeting at the top of the stairs, when I promise them that much fun awaits us the next day, I retreat back down to the kitchen to catch up with our hosts. We laugh in the toasty warmth of the woodstove, and Warren and I offer up tales of our adventures on Monhegan.

But that night, despite the cheery conversation, sometime after we climb into bed, something starts to shift for Warren and me. Never mind that mushy, overwhelming, in-love sensation from the night before and how I swore I'd cling to it and remind myself of it forever, maybe even especially during hard relationship moments. Clearly I was heavily delusional. For now, here, with no fanfare, comes still more living proof of how protracted can be the death of an old habit like, say, engaging in petty arguments with one's partner. This about face inside of a mere 24 hours no less.

The argument does not begin as an argument, but rather a discussion. We happen to be assigned a full-size bed, perfectly adequate for many couples the world over. Warren and I just happen to not be one of those couples. In fact, we have been through more beds and bed configurations in our years together than any other couple I know. When early on he complained my full-sized bed was too small— because unlike me, the ultimate spooner, Warren is a do-not-touch-me-with-your-body-or-your-blankets-or-even-your-breath-when-I-am-sleeping type— I proposed buying a queen mattress. His frugality cried out in anguish at the folly of this suggestion. Back to square one: complaining.

Once, fed up with his bellyaching, and more fed up with his refusal to let money solve the problem as I proposed, I stormed off to buy a new bed with money I didn't have. At the mattress store, it dawned on me that to buy a queen would mean a need for queen bedding. So to save at least a little money, I just got another full-sized bed and crammed it into my room beside the bed already in there. One bed frame turned out to be higher than the other, recalling the crowded beach house of my childhood, which, to accommodate our gigantic brood, featured beds of all sizes and heights smooshed into all available corners, even the kitchen. Warren and I actually enjoyed this setup immensely, and pretended for a spell that we were at sleep-away camp.

Then there was the time, also fed up, I took this same full-sized mattress, by now known as Warren's Bed, and put it in the spare room, to "punish" him for being a pain-in-the-ass sleeper and, more importantly, to commemorate another proposed breakup. Talk about irony. That move saved the relationship. He exalted in this Virginia Woolfian turn of events, was delighted he could now sleep without risking any danger that I or my top sheet might accidentally brush up against him in the night.

That arrangement lasted awhile, until I said he could either pony up the dough for a queen mattress or could find someone else to torture with his bizarre sleeping idiosyncrasies. He promised the bed but then procrastination kicked in. Fed up for a third time, I headed to IKEA to find a cheap frame in the Dent & Sale room to match the queen-sized mattress a friend's sister bequeathed me. Ultimately this is what we settled for, and what settled us, but not before I nearly gouged my eyes out in a fit of rage as I attempted to assemble the frame, using only the bobby-pin-sized Allen wrench in the bottom of the box and some instructions that combined illustrations more rudimentary than a Ziggy cartoon with text translated from Romanian to English by someone who knew neither language (and, in fact, gave the distinct impression of not knowing any language at all).

But here we are now, back to Rectangle One, a full-sized bed. Warren reverts to complain mode. "Scoot over!" He admonishes me verbally first, then attempts to physically nudge me to the outer edge of the mattress.

I hiss at him in the dark to shut up, this bed is just fine, thank you very much. He wakes me up at irritating intervals during the night— irritating intervals being for me any stretch fewer than seven hours. Even in my groggy state, the deep anxiety that informs my waking life takes over and my brain shoots in three distinct directions, until at last I can discern the word in the overlapping section of the Venn diagram these looping thoughts form: *WORRY!*

On the one hand, I worry about Warren's discomfort. This I get from my mom, the queen of selflessness, from whom I learned to serve my man by watching her serve hers. Even when I don't want to serve, even when I fight it, and make conscious notes to not cater, there will forever be a way deeper tug that tells me to care for others first, just like she taught me through her role modeling.

Not just Warren, either. Anyone. Once, when Henry was very little and in a jogger stroller, I "parked" him to run to the bottom of a small hill to help a struggling, wheelchair-bound stranger ascend the incline. All well and good, except I left my child in a rolling vehicle on a decline and yes, the stroller rolled. And no, thankfully he did not go sailing into traffic. But yes, to this day— two decades later— I cannot drive by that spot without remembering that good deeds really do risk big punishment.

On the other hand, I also worry about our hosts' feelings. Wouldn't it upset them and insult them to know that Warren aka Goldilocks is anything but purely grateful for this mattress they've provided us? This concern really gets the old monkey mind going as I project myself far into the next day, and try to imagine how I might handle it if our hosts beg us to stay another night. *"Sorry, but Warren will only stay if you go buy a bed that is at least eight feet by nine feet!"*

Then there is the third hand: *I AM TRYING TO FUCKING SLEEP HERE, WARREN. AND YOU ARE BEING A BIG FAT BABY!* Because here's the thing about me when I am asleep— even though I can wake up in a second (thank you motherhood, thank you PTSD-induced hyper vigilance), that doesn't mean I *like* being awakened, or that I am particularly *pleasant* when stirred from a deep slumber. Fact is, wake me up abruptly and odds are beyond excellent that I will be a total bitch.

Warren, who almost only ever sleeps for four hours at a stretch, followed by several hours awake, then a few asleep, plus naps throughout the day, seems unable to grasp the concept of the eight-hour snooze. We have worked hard to honor our very different sleeping styles— for example when he wakes up, he'll go in the other room and watch something on the computer and use the headphones so as not to wake me.

But there are still times when he cannot resist creeping back into bed and staring at me— not in quiet adoration but in eager anticipation of my return to consciousness, very much like my one-hundred-plus pound Labrador, Dante, likes to do. Even in my deepest sleep, it doesn't take long for me to sense when another being— maybe a dog, maybe Warren— is beside me telepathing an eager message of hope: *"Is it time to wake up yet? Wanna wake up? Will you wake up? I wonder when you'll wake up?!"*

Sometimes I give in and wake up. Often these shared, pre-dawn moments are our funniest, our brains relaxed, puns flying, silliness abounding. But then, before long, my being awake seems to have a tryptophanic effect and Warren will conk out, leaving me alone in full consciousness (I'm not good at resuming sleep).

At Vince and Diana's, by about the fourth time Warren wakes me, I'm done with trying to resume sleeping. I can hear the kids in the other room. I can smell the coffee. So I get up, far too early, and try to stuff my irritation at being sleep-deprived. The kids' delight at our reunion helps. Still, I am quietly recalling and storing up details from my Night of Many Interruptions, saving them for a later argument I can't help but start planning, ostensibly to help Warren learn how to "better communicate for the sake of the relationship," but really, I know, to rip him a new one for not behaving in the precise manner I wish for him to behave.

We haven't argued much, not in a few days. And, relative to how frequently we used to argue in our early days together, we are regular Ambassadors of Shalom these days. Still, like plants need rain, like ticks need blood, like puppies need to pee in the house, sometimes we seem to need to go at it. The mattress incident, as it will turn out, will only be foreshadowing to a much bigger rift. Before forty-eight hours pass, we will find ourselves in a real, roof-rattling, foot-stomping, top-o-the-lungs screaming match, a total mess.

But first, there is much joy to be had, and this comes courtesy of Diana and the kids.

Chapter Fourteen

Of course my waking up (too early) and exiting the smaller-than-he-prefers bed allows Warren to fall into a sound sleep. In the next room, a large open space that combines living area and big kitchen, Diana is working on her bread again and the kids are eating breakfast. I settle in with some coffee and, for the moment, my Warren irritation melts away. These kids are so amazing, so wide-eyed, so inquisitive and so utterly unsullied by the world's bullshit that, as with their mother, it's as if they dwell in another century.

I'm not talking about precious or naïve. I'm just saying that, thanks to their parents' influence, their life focus is pointed in quite a different direction than so many other children. To wit: they invite me to join them outside to feed the chickens and gather eggs. They don't eat processed crap. And when I give them the gift I've brought them— a drop spindle so they can make their own yarn— I get the sort of delighted reaction that, to elicit such from another sort of child, might require something along the lines of an iPad or an Xbox, not a simple wooden device that requires hard work to yield results.

Then Warren wakes up, and the real fun begins. I am further able to delay the brewing argument because he arrives in the kitchen game for games, ready to be one of the kids. This has been perhaps the biggest the blessing and yet an occasional curse of life with Warren. When I met him, as I emerged from my divorce, when life felt so unbearably heavy and all I did was cry, being in the presence of a perpetual fourteen-year-old trapped in a man's body was a very good thing. There was no need for serious conversation and the constant silliness greatly contributed to my healing.

But at a certain point— how does that old country song go? Something about how he married her because he thought she'd never change and she married him because she thought he would? — I found myself sometimes craving more serious conversations, less farting in public. And while he has always proved beyond competent during crises and emergencies, in our day-to-day living good luck trying to get him to even feign gravitas. In truth I'd rather live with a jester than a king any day, though during certain discussions (read: arguments), I have found myself futilely (and, okay, sometimes childishly) demanding he set his childish behavior aside.

Not today. Today Warren's perpetual-youth perspective dovetails nicely with the opportunities at hand. He is not just going to act like a child for the benefit of the actual children. No, he *is* one of them. And now that all we're all awake, I get out the book I've brought to share with Fiona and Peter. It's written in German, a *kinder* book about a mole with a big mound of shit on his head, who is trying to figure out how the shit got there. (In truth, I originally acquired this book for Warren, knowing he would love it.)

Diana stands at her island counter, like a teacher at the head of the class, while the Fiona and Peter sit rapt on stools across from her. The more she reads about the shit-headed mole, the harder she laughs, and the more we laugh, at least as much at her joy as the hilarious illustrations.

Then it's off to the barn out back, where the kids give Warren and me a tour of the drafty old structure, upstairs and down. Then they produce a couple of scooters, get us situated on a pair of folding chairs, and explain the rules of a variation on Red Light, Green Light they have created. They will scooter around the barn as fast as they can, orbiting us, whizzing out of sight into the other rooms and then back close to us. We will call out, "Red light!" or "Green light!" to make them stop and start.

They scoot and scoot and scoot and Warren and I sit in our chairs and I knit as Warren, not content with a mere two options, invents more and more intricate, ridiculously silly rules.

"Yellow!" Warren yells, and the kids have to stop, get off the scooters, and carry them, continuing on foot around the barn. "Brown!" he shouts, a cue to go backwards. They love this. I love this, too, love it for the reminder of how funny and utterly silly Warren can be, how easily he can tap into the minds of kids and know just how to engage them. And I love it for other reasons— here I am, sitting in an old barn in the middle of a weekday, far from my computer and iPhone, just knitting and laughing.

Though we are sitting still and the kids are zooming around, they wear us out first. We announce it's time to return to the house. Reluctantly they agree, scheming as we tromp back over what we should do next.

Back inside, the kids decide a game of Monopoly is in order. The slumlording commences, and with it a keen view (at least by my estimation) into the minds and hearts of each of the five of us playing. Warren signs on as banker (not a surprise) and he and Diana will prove to be the most cutthroat among us, getting sucked in and hypnotized by the promise of winning, if only attention is paid and strategies duly executed. Fiona wants to buy everything she can get her hands on (a girl after my own heart). And Peter winds up mortgaging a lot of his property in the interest of maintaining liquidity.

Me? I really don't care. Not as in I am apathetic about playing with the kids— for this I feel enthusiasm. But I don't give a rat's ass about winning. Something in this game is mirroring my real life attitude of late: I just can't get that interested in money, in what it takes to get ahead. Playing is enough for me, just staying afloat, enjoying what I have, not sweating the losses.

At certain points I even get distracted, feel a pull to go and sit down and do some work, check some email, be alone in my bubble. I pull out my iPhone from time to time, sneak a glance at incoming notes, pull up a photo to illustrate some story I am telling in stops and starts over the multiple conversations happening across the board. Fiona is instantly entranced by the device and quickly figures out how to scroll through my photo album. She asks how so many pictures can fit into such a slim container, reminding me of when Henry once announced, "The Beatles are inside our radio, Mom!"

Diana has a pet cockatiel, Frank, who enjoys free-range flight throughout the house. Harriett, the family dog, with hair like Chewbacca and a blind eye clouded over milky, is the sole focus of Frank's attention. For you see, Frank is, I say without exaggeration, passionately in love with Harriett. Beyond in love. Infatuated. *Obsessed.* And so wherever Harriett goes, Frank follows, flapping his way across the room, lighting on her back, trying to nest in her tangle of Wookie fur.

Harriett is stunningly tolerant of this behavior for the most part, though she has her moments, faux-snapping at Frank whom, given his obsession and proximity, surely Harriett could eat. She doesn't. She does let him know when to back off. This goes on all day. Harriett, arthritically hobbling across the room, curling in a ball on her dog bed. Frank, heart and wings aflutter, in hot pursuit, nestling on Harriett's back. Harriett snapping. Frank taking a few steps away, down off Harriett's back, but close enough to stand guard so that if any of us approach Harriett, Frank will be near enough to chastise us loudly.

We break for lunch, then more Monopoly, more unrequited bird/dog love, more laughter, more pictures. Then the kids take me outside to gather more eggs and to play numerous variations of tag. Color tag, freeze tag, fox and rabbit tag. All these versions are new to me, but they share a common, easy-to-spot theme: no matter what type of tag we are playing, I will lose. The kids are fast, they are inexhaustible and they are giggling their heads off as I lope-saunter-stagger across the lawn. They never get winded. I feel like a visit to the ER might soon be in order.

Our day is not interrupted by school bells or TV shows or other outside influences. We make our own fun, and what fun we have. Chalk up another day mostly away from the computer. I squeeze in just a little work here and there, respond to a few work-related emails. But I am relearning life before the Technology Revolution, and— not that I need to find a lesson in every game of Monopoly or tag— I am paying close attention to the false sense of urgency I attach to my work, the amount of complaining I do about not ever having enough time, and to the life my friends are living up here in small-town Maine. Ideas and theories are forming. Vague resolutions are knocking at the door. Could I ever slow down? Do I really want to?

The afternoon starts heading in the direction of evening, and the plan is that once Vince gets back, we'll say goodbye and be on our way. The night before we asked Vince and Diana to help us pick a next destination, someplace we might see a moose and some vivid autumn colors. Our hosts debated, mulled, tossed out suggestions, and finally urged us to go to Mooseville, a couple of hours east, spitting distance from the Canadian border.

Vince arrives home near dusk, dressed in his work duds. He stands in the kitchen, giving us a lecture about the dangers of hormonal adolescent bull moose, and some unwanted details of what happens if a car collides with one. Hint: the height of a moose is so great that when one comes crashing through your windshield, you most certainly will be a goner.

Look at Vince. Listen to him. He grew up. I grew up. We are nearly fifty now, a number that sounds rather big, though I still feel sixteen in my heart. But even when he was young Vince was at least a little bit old. And even though he engaged in some of the same all-night idiocy as the rest of us, something about him always struck me as mature and in-charge. In our young twenties, when I was alternately reading women's mags and Bukowski and listening to power pop, Vince was devouring the *New York Times* and listening intently to the Oliver North hearings on NPR. He had a great interest in politics from a very young age, and more than a couple of related opinions he was happy— gleeful— to share.

The serious side, the maturity, is still present and there is more of it. His tone as he explains about the moose is stern, though not mean. His genuine concern reminds me of something very important about him: Pigsty abandonments and momentarily broken heart notwithstanding, I think I always knew that I could rely on Vince in an emergency, understood he would be the keep-calm-and-carry-on sort, that I could call him from the middle of Pennsylvania and he would, if necessary, drive all night from West Virginia to change my cracked distributor cap.

Looking back now over twenty-five years, probably what fascinated me most was that Vince knew how to take care of himself, and to do so with a sense of confidence. When we met, in Knoxville, it's true I'd already been on my own for five years or so, and had my own place, and a job. Maybe to some I appeared to be confident and independent. But inside there was more than a little turmoil. I was drunk often, had no concept of money management, and desperately flung myself at one unrequited crush after another. My writing was not very good, which I know now is to be expected of most twenty-three year-olds. But I was hungry to get somewhere, destination not entirely known, only that arriving should magically involve a small fortune and some measure of fame.

Don't let me be too hard on myself here, though. Knoxville 1987, when Vince and I met, remains fixed in my Museum of Memories as a place of wonder. Even though I can still see myself in any number of ugly scenes— drunk and smashing a beer bottle on the ground in anger upon being told by my landlord I was being kicked out for too many loud parties, watching my alleged best friend sashay off to fuck the guy she knew I desperately pined for— I can also see more than a few flashes of magic.

Over the years I have sometimes fantasized about moving back to Knoxville. Once I actually did go back for a couple of months to heal from my first divorce, but that was predetermined to be temporary respite. Any longing I've ever had to go back permanently though, I have tempered with a reality check. I know that the urge is not so much to return to that little city, but to go back in time to the place in my life where I was learning, not easily, how to be a grown up.

Me and my little coffee pot and my string of dumpy apartments. Me and my no-mattress bedroom and bringing one-night stands home to roll around on the floor. Me quitting my day job as an editorial assistant to waitress by day and write freelance by night. Me taking the stage at The Vatican Pizza, delivering my bad poetry to a small crowd, drunk and cheering. Me hanging out with my friend Kevin, who later on down the line, would move back to St. Louis, and, when I visited him there, would introduce me to his beautiful red-headed brother— the man with whom eventually I'd have my amazing son— the two of us falling in love through the letters we sent back and forth. Me, walking to the Knoxville post office, my Walkman headphones blasting Leonard Cohen's *I'm Your Man*, as I dropped off or picked up (often both) another letter for or from Big Red.

Knoxville represents so much for me. And Vince, though he's been gone from that place longer than me, represents Knoxville. Looking at him, I see not precisely a mirror, but still a sort of reflection. There we were, here we are. There is no logical explanation in the world for what sparked our interest in one another all those years ago— to say our differences far outweighed our similarities is an understatement. Maybe the lives of the adolescent bull moose can shed some light here. Maybe hormones get to take all the credit. Maybe our path crossing was more of a crash than a calculation.

But no. There was something else. Because there are plenty of people I knew then that I don't know now. Vince and I have chosen to stay in touch for some other reason. I don't even need to spend time puzzling over the *whys* of the reason. I'm just glad I have this witness to my youth, a witness who also got to watch me slowly become who I am. And I'm glad now, to be invited into Vince's home, to have the chance to laugh with his wife and play tag with his kids.

Screech. Brake slam. Oh god, am I sounding like one of those fucking *Chicken Soup for the Soul* books? I am. Let me try again, and explain it in the punk rock terms of my youth. I was so fucking fucked up when Vince met me, lost in my heart, lost in the booze. I hardly knew my head from my ass, though I put up a good front, at least I thought I did. And by some miracle, we both lived this long, and now I get to see him and have his kids wear my ass out running in the yard, and bankrupt me at the Monopoly board, and when I grow up I want to be his wife, by which I do not mean *I* want to be *with* Vince, but rather I want to *be* Diana, because she can spin and knit amazing things and bake delicious bread and raise delightful kids—human and goat variety, both—and, well to sum it up, she's just a total bad ass.

There, that's better.

Not a fan of goodbyes, I do the awkward thing in the driveway, thanks and hugs all around, promises to come back soon. Vince and Diana offer a few more warnings about Bullwinkle's evil cousins lurking all around us. Now I am fully terrified, the sky is darkening, and the rain has started up again. *Oh goody.* Two hours of wet winding roads with teen boy moose, like Whac-a-Moles on steroids, just waiting to pop out of the woods and into the front seat of Shitty Shitty Putt Putt, which will not have anywhere near enough power to beat them back into the spaces from whence they came. I grip the wheel tightly, as if this action will serve as a sort of talisman— the White-Knuckled Moose Repellent Maneuver!

As the sky gets darker still, and the rain falls harder still, we wend our way up toward Mooseville, the town that soon will become permanently embedded in our collection of stories that fall under the umbrella of fights that are so preposterous they actually can be classified as hilarious but not until at least a couple months have passed. I still think it started, the seed of it, when Warren started whining the night before about his princess and the pea bullshit with the "too small mattress." But that's easy for me to say, as I am captain of this keyboard.

Warren would no doubt chalk it up to one of his many utterly infuriating theories, the main one being that we humans are nothing but big beakers of chemicals, and that those chemicals are bound to have reactions, and that you just have to wait for the fizzing to subside. I am a fan of yelling at him that this notion is the ultimate bullshit, that our feelings are *REAL GODDAMMIT.* To which, if his chemicals/feelings are in just the right precarious place, he will respond that the feelings are nothing more but part of the chemistry set to which he is referring.

He says all this, I think, mostly to get a rise out of me. Which I then accuse him of doing. At which point he then denies my accusation by stating that he is simply speaking a truth, the facts, implying (to my ears) that I am irrational. Then, I, needing to have the last word (of course), will call him Rainman and tell him he is, once again, exhibiting Asperger's traits, and *MAYBE HE FUCKING NEEDS TO GET THAT DIAGNOSED AND FUCKING TAKEN CARE OF.*

But we're not there yet. First, we have to finish the drive, and get to the hotel, where we will find more beds for Warren to decry, thus setting the stage for something so much bigger, so much more dramatic, so much louder than any exchange we've engaged in in a very, very long time.

Chapter Fifteen

I am on super high alert for sinister moose. I drive and drive, and my eyes dart to and fro, trying to peer into the pitch-black woods that line the small road we are crawling along. As if I might actually spot a charging moose in time, halt the vehicle, avert collision.

A couple of hours later, we pull up to the Mooseville Inn, a place so quaint and historic that it is depicted on the website not in a photograph, but in an old-timey illustration. I love the look of it, love that we will be again stepping back time, just as we did at Monhegan House.

But wait. I didn't look closely enough. Yes, the Mooseville Inn really is an historic edifice. Yes, as you might expect, the original structure features a lobby packed with massive taxidermied mammals, including a bear upright and ready to pounce, and a moose head, roughly the size of Delaware, protruding from the wall, creepy enough in its disembodied state and creepier still thanks to lighting that casts diabolic shadows all around it. But the Mooseville Inn has a subtitle— Motor Lodge— that I didn't notice when searching online for a place to stay. It is to this far more recently constructed motel around back that we are relegated, as the main building has been commandeered, *in toto,* by a group of touring senior citizens, those elder bastards!

The desk clerk is kind enough, and hands us our key and a bag of muffins to get us started the next morning. We pull the Kia around back. Before we even exit the car we are both laying bets we don't want to win that our quarters on the back forty will hardly match the elegance promised by the main building. Sadly, we win.

No, the room is not a total dump. But for $120 per night, I really hoped for amenities like, you know, a soap dish in the shower, an actual toilet paper dispenser, that sort of thing.

Warren doesn't mince words. "We paid how much for this?" he asks. And this comment immediately puts me in the uncomfortable place of defending our rather dumpy room. Why defend it? Why not hop on board the disgust train and have fun picking apart the dingy rug, the schlumpy feel of this place? Actually, I can answer that question. As ever, though, I insist on taking the long route. Ready?

Once upon a time, not long after my first divorce, from the ether emerged a man I hadn't heard from since my Knoxville days, a decade earlier. At the time I was on ill-prescribed Prozac and still drinking heavily— neither of these a good standalone choice for me, the combined effect exponentially worse still. The pills and booze constituted two-thirds of a losing trifecta that also included my post-divorce emotional vulnerability. Thus I was in a state that included constant weeping, a perpetual hangover, and a speeded-up metabolism that inspired massive weight loss and an unquenchable desire to play tennis every day, though I was far too spaced out to actually keep track of the score. In Drew— he with his endless emails confessing a long-ago crush he now felt rekindling— I found escapism and hope. The plan was simple— with his wit he could rescue me from my divorce grief, and with his daunting manliness (the dude was 6'5") he could quell the fear inspired by my ex-husband's stalking!

So wrapped up in this fantasy did I become, I even managed to convince myself that Drew's favorite pastime— playing the role of King in his local branch of the Society for Creative Anachronism— was sort of neato! Did I really believe this? Hindsight is begging me to think and claim otherwise, but I admit I have always had a bad habit of drumming up enthusiasm for whatever passion one potential beau or another possesses, even if those passions involved, say, Wiffle ball bats wrapped in tin foil as some sort of representation of medieval weaponry.

When I finally visited Drew for a week of heavy drinking punctuated by one or two truly awful sexual encounters and several heated arguments (apparently I had grown "too feminist" for his liking in our years apart), any tolerance-cum-"excitement" I had whipped up over the whole SCA thing turned to mortification when he took me to a park to watch him in action. There, his lieges, the whole lot of them dressed in tunics, had to kneel before their king and beseech him, in Ye Fake Olde Englishe, for the privilege of a duel, to be conducted using aforementioned "swords."

Mortified to be associated with this preposterous embrace of the Middle Ages, I sat on the hood of Drew's car, buried my head in a screenplay I was reading, and feigned non-association. This did not please milord, and our already strained "relationship" sank deeper into a black hole of despair, despair fueled by the knowledge that I could not afford to change my return flight and sally forth more swiftly back to the place from whence I'd come, the evil kingdom of equality-embracing sassy lassies who, by Drew's estimation, probably should be, for their own good, locked up in a tower for all of eternity and then some.

At long last, safely ensconced back in Austin, serving up this tale in my kitchen to my horrified and wildly amused friends, I got to the part about SCA attire and my friend Robert, literally recoiling several steps, intoned in his deep voice, "You didn't tell me he wore a *dress*!"

That comment, and the way in which Robert delivered it, prompted in me the same urge that visits me now as Warren and I scrutinize our room in Mooseville. In reality, as I agreed with Robert's criticism of Drew, I agree with Warren's assessment of this borderline dump. On principle though, because I made the choice in question— to fuck the king, to rent this room— I feel personally attacked, and thus left in that weird position of wanting to stand up for the very thing of which I am hardly a fan myself.

My earlier irritation with Warren creeps back in. He tries to explain he isn't insulting *me*, but I have a hard time buying this proclamation. Yes, he is right, this place is hardly worth the money we've laid out, but, too, isn't this also yet another case of his frugality being at the heart of the complaint? *Can't he just fucking relax and roll with it for once, goddammit?*

Though I cannot see it now, later I will come to understand this moment as containing one of those great, utterly undeniable, That Which I Hate to Admit details: *Doesn't it have to be true that if Warren has certain characteristics that drive me nuts on a regular basis, then I, too, must have certain characteristics that drive him nuts, also on a regular basis?* And if the answer to this is *yes* (and fucking shit crap hell, the answer *is* yes), then if I spend so much time wishing he would adjust his attitude, does this not entitle him to similar wishing regarding me? And if I do not wish to change, say, my propensity for reacting strongly to the world, then mustn't I allow him similar leeway such as his right to be frugal and, furthermore, to be vocal about his frugality?

Well, yes, I suppose so. But these are only things I can contemplate alone in a room, long after the fact. The bridge between knowledge and application continues to be one that proves difficult to navigate for me, and utterly impossible in the heat of the moment, in the presence of He Who Currently Seems to Exist Solely to Irritate the Shit Out of Me.

I fall asleep pretty quickly, exhausted from Moosewatch 2011 and pouting from Warren's lack of appreciation for this room that I also don't appreciate but cannot, out of stubbornness, admit to not appreciating.

Tonight we are sleeping in separate beds not out of anger, though there is that, but because this is something else that helps when we travel together. For all the bellyaching I do about wanting to sleep together and spoon and wake up slowly entwined in one another's arms like a mythical mermaid and merman drifting to the surface of wakefulness, the truth is that when one sleeps alone, one sleeps better. That even holds for me and the dogs. While I am prone to insist that the comfort factor, both physical and psychological, of having all four of my beasts heaped on me in a puppy pile aids my restfulness, I know from experimenting that nights they spend on the couch, I wake up feeling much more refreshed the next day. (Please don't tell them I said this).

The night of solid sleep makes a difference for the better. I wake up early, brew up the in-house, liquid-feces-like beverage being offered up as "coffee" in the crappy plastic coffee pot, and slurp it down, trying to stay focused on gratitude for caffeine within reach. I eat the muffin bestowed upon me the night before. I wonder to myself, *What's the best way to find a real, live moose, one that will gracefully amble by the car without actually bursting through the windshield?*

I decide to investigate, strolling the short distance between the motor lodge portion of the inn and over to the actual inn, the few yards making all the difference between ugly, semi-functional modern day "architecture" and elegant historic design. As I step up on the porch, to my surprise and delight I run into a cheerful man weighed down by an enormous moose antler, which he is nonchalantly carrying, like it's the morning paper or a small sack lunch. Delivering my question in what I hope will clearly come across as feigned stupidity, I ask, "Will you please tell me where to find a moose?"

Not missing a beat, he grins and answers, "Sure! Hire a guide!" Would that I had taken his joke seriously and hired him on the spot. How differently the day surely would have turned out. Instead we laugh, then he tells me he's just taken a group out and they'd spotted a couple of moose. He points vaguely in a direction I won't be able to remember later, says they were "over there," and off he strolls, lugging the antler.

I return to the Bates Motel section of the property and retrieve Warren, and together we head back to the lobby of the real inn, where we are accosted by the hotel owner who cheerfully invites us to partake in the buffet being served in the dining room.

Time for a lesson in mixed signals. Best as I can tell, the buffet, now but dregs of eggs in chilling chafing dishes, their Sterno flames dwindling to mere receding tongues of blue, has been thoroughly picked over by the group of silver-haired moose seekers. Knowing it will please Warren to, in a manner of speaking, recoup some of our room fee by demolishing what remains and thus saving on the price of breakfast out, I agree we should dig in.

Warren, it should be noted, is a very good eater. That's actually a nickname he was been given long ago, when some friend's mother, noting his overflowing and then later polished off plate, proclaimed, "Warren is a good eater!" At the buffet, he piles on the bacon, the toast, the mini muffins.

We sit to eat and here comes the waiter, rather formally dressed, to offer us fresh juice and made-to-order eggs. Warren and I look at each other. They would give us fresh cooked eggs on the house? Maybe we haven't made a mistake coming here! So we order some eggs.

As we wait, Warren has a thought. "They're going to charge us for those eggs," he speculates.

"No way," I say, both reflexively— a day without countering each other being unthinkable— and sincerely. I have very clearly picked up the message in the owner's tone that he is making a big-hearted gesture. Nobody would actually charge for the cold leftovers of another group's buffet.

Or would they?

Well, at least we grow very full. So when The Very Formal Waiter hits us with a check for $30, we begrudgingly concur that the owner is, no doubt, a very good salesman. A younger me might've threatened to return my breakfast to the plate and declare I'd been duped. But vengeful bulimia seems an unkind route to take and, worse, would leave me hungry all over again. So we take our lumps, pay our stupid check, and set out to find us a moose.

Rain continues to fall. It isn't a hard rain but by this point in the trip any notion I'd had of hiking my way to slimmer thighs in seven days is gone. I love walking. I try my best to walk at least three miles every day. When I set off on this journey thinking I'd be hiking, I wasn't fooling myself. But the relentless rain, even in its lighter form as today, inspires in me a candy-ass lethargy. I might get chilly. I might stay damp all day. Excuse. Excuse. Excuse. We drive off, bellies fuller, wallets lighter, and bodies unexercised, in a direction Warren has decided will yield a moose sighting.

We drive and we drive and then we drive some more. We keep driving. We drive some more. The leaves have begun to turn, some of the trees offering show-stopping displays of insane, eye-burning dazzlement. We talk. We laugh. We have a new inside joke to entertain us— the "free" $30 breakfast. *Hahahaha! Free! Hahahaha!*

And then we spot him! Well, I spot him, and just his ass. *"A MOOSE!"* I shout. Warren looks up just in time as Bullwinkle traipses off into the forest. Excellent. Now we can check moose-sighting and leaf-gawking off our list. Should we add a bonus goal, try to cross over into Canada? I feel half-game but Warren doesn't want to go that far. We keep driving along at our meandering pace.

At a hunting and fishing outfitter in a small town along the way, we pull in. I am hoping for a moose t-shirt which, when coupled with the moose shirt I already own, would then qualify me as a fledgling collector. I love moose. Adore them. The passion is not entirely random— my nickname as a teenager, at least as far as one of my older sisters was concerned, was *Moose*. Her reasoning was that since, at 5'5" and 120 pounds, I was the tallest and heaviest of eight sisters, I was the moose.

I can't find a moose shirt that suits me. The pickings are slimmer than you might expect in moose country. The store is empty save for Warren and me, and no matter how much I've worked to train myself that one is not obliged to buy something just because one is the only shopper, I can't walk away empty-handed.

Up and down the aisles I trudge, *oohing* and *ahhing* at the taxidermied menagerie lining the shelves, glaring down from the walls, freeze-framed on shelves in positions of prowl. I tear my real eyes away from their glass ones long enough to peruse the Made-in-China tchotchkes stamped MAINE, trying to settle on the one that will be heading back to Texas with me. And then, I see him.

"*LOOK!*" I squeal at Warren. "*LOOK LOOK!*" A bobble-headed dashboard moose, coated in faux suede, waiting to be activated. I reach out and lightly tap his little moose head. As if to assure me that my choice is the right one, he instantly gives a nod, and then another and another. You might argue that bobble-heads, by their nature, nod. I would tell you your argument is lost on me and quit being such a buzzkill. I'm telling you, *that specific moose nodded specifically at me.*

The Kia feels a thousand times better once we get the moose situated on the front dash. I know his name almost instantly, the way some new parents swear they can see an infant's name written on its face as it exits the birth canal. "He's Yeah the Affirmative Moose!" I announce

"Yeah!" says Warren.

"Yeah!" I agree.

Yeah nods his approval, and continues to nod for the next hour or so, as if he is in on all the silly jokes we are sharing now that my mood has lifted and I am distracted from the petty disagreement over the cost of our room and from indignation at having been duped into a $30 brunch. But then, with no warning, thanks to some little comment, happiness yields to unhappiness and now Yeah appears to be mocking us. It gets so bad that Yeah must be punished for his sarcastic attitude, must be banished to the backseat, his body separated from his mocking head. *That'll teach you, Yeah!*

How does the argument start? Do you really want to know that? You do, don't you? I would have to say it starts with my full bladder or, more precisely, my foolish choice to announce I have a full bladder.

Though I can't remember this myself, I believe Warren when he reminds me— whenever I tell the story I am about to tell here— that earlier in the day, as we were driving along those back roads, with gas stations few and far between, we stopped so I could pee in the grass. Totally believable. I'm not opposed to squatting when absolutely necessary, and any shred of modesty I had fell by the wayside back during Henry's homebirth in 1990, which turned into an emergency and thus found my house full of cops and ambulance drivers who all witnessed me pushing out the placenta on the heels of a massive fart.

But for whatever reason, when I find myself again with a full bladder on this autumn day as we drive closer and closer to the Canadian border, I do not wish to repeat my earlier method of relief. I want an actual pot into which to piss. And it's quite possible that the main reason I wish for such is simply because Warren suggests, repeatedly, that we just pull over again.

Have I emphasized enough the component of resistance that exists, like some unique entity, some inexorable poltergeist, between us? At our worst (some friends might say "most hilarious," while others would say "most discomforting") we can take this resistance game to vertigo-inducing heights. I could say, "The sky is blue," and, reflexively, Warren will refute me instantly— "No it's not. It's plaid!" Similarly, he could point out that a patch of dirt is just as good as a porcelain throne for the dispensing of urine, and even if he is utterly correct, I might just not be able to stop myself from an unmediated, *"Nunh-uh!"*

So it goes this afternoon. Maybe we are really just weary of one another's company, a common pitfall of 24/7 togetherness, particularly given our at-home dynamic of (carefully planned and greatly appreciated) separate houses and regularly scheduled full days apart as a matter of course. Maybe we have cabin fever.

Whatever pulls the trigger, the explosion is swift and loud. All laughter at Yeah's perpetually bobbing head stops. Warren has asked me one time too many if I want to pull over, and he has asked me one time too many another question, ironic given my screaming bladder: Do I want some of his water?

DO I WANT WATER? DO I WANT WATER WHEN MY BLADDER IS ABOUT TO BURST? NO I DO NOT WANT ANY OF YOUR STUPID FUCKING WATER!

That is, more or less, the thought bubble floating over my head like a storm cloud. I apply the brakes, not hard enough to jolt us forward, but enough to come to a full stop rather quickly. I believe I do this "to be funny."

But how can I think this will be funny? What devil invades our minds during moments like these, when we reach into our bag of cheap and dirty tricks and pull out the one we know will most aggravate our partner and then, worse, decide to execute the trick and, worst of all, rationalize that *it will be funny*? Long ago Warren had decried this tendency of mine to come to an unannounced, unnecessary, complete stop— five feet from his driveway for instance— in order to deliver a lecture.

As I halt Shitty Shitty Putt Putt, Yeah nods. It is this particular nod that merits him being sent to the backseat, where he will be left, out of sight and out of nod. Warren— now at least as irritated as me— raises his voice. Raises his voice? *RAISES HIS VOICE?* Have we not gone over this, for four years now, that a raised voice shuts me down? (Well, I mean, *his* raised voice because yes, I, hypocrite, certainly am allowed raise my own voice.)

There is an invisible moment, a nanosecond, less than a nanosecond. We go from *before* (laughing, silly, punning, creating a back story for Yeah) to *after*. After is a very ugly place. We are off to the Anger Races and there is no stopping us. The louder Warren gets, the more I protest. The more I protest, the more he protests back. If the nature of an argument could magically render the participants to the size and attire the maturity level of their disagreement most reflects, Warren and I would find ourselves emerging from a big puff of smoke, shrunken down to about three-feet tall, decked out in Garanimals or Baby Gap outfits, tugging back and forth on an innocent Teddy Bear symbolic of our folly.

No magic here, though. Just two alleged adults, our combined age approximately ninety, unable to control ourselves. I can't pinpoint what black bile spews from my own piehole, not because I am a fan of the "I-don't-recall" strategy, but because my job in the moment is not to monitor the rote shit I am spilling— probably something including the words *asshole* and *dumb ass* and *fucking bullshit!*— but more to focus on Warren's ugly verbal arsenal, so I can indignantly feel the burn of his words, and also save them up for later, recall them in future arguments, hurl them right back at him—*"Remember that time in Maine when you were such an ass and called me blahtity blah blah blah?!! REMEMBER THAT?!!"*

Warren does not disappoint, letting loose a few warm-up shots before whipping out his big gun and firing pointblank. *"YOU NEED FUCKING THERAPY!"* he hollers.

Therapy? *Really*, Warren? THERAPY?

"I LOVE THERAPY YOU DUMBASS!" I yell, or words to those effect. I'm the one who goes around telling everyone the wonders of therapy. Why do men pull this one out on women? Why do they issue the need for therapy as a threat? My father used to threaten me with therapy and had I but an inkling of the wonders of such, I would've dared him to follow through.

We yell some more. Then I get an idea. I know just where this idea comes from, because, as noted, I have done centuries of therapy, where I learned, among other things, that not only is therapy not a punishment and also not something to be stigmatized, but that therapy can really help you sort shit out. Such as that I am prone to inhabiting one of four psychological roles—Helpless Baby, Angry Adolescent, Inner Critic, Wise Woman—that, combined, make up the whole of me.

I am, with all certainty, in full on *Angry Adolescent* mode here. Warren is yelling and I am feeling defensive and all I can do is fight back but wait, no… There is another choice! It dawns on me in an instant. I can walk away! I can walk away not in a mature fashion, but in fury and spite. I can tell him that if he doesn't shut up *RIGHT THIS MINUTE* then I am going to *GET OUT OF THE CAR AND WALK BACK TO AUSTIN, TEXAS, RIGHT NOW!*

So there I sit, hands gripping the wheel, my rage toward Warren past fever pitch and heading into roiling lava. I can see the words in my head, know that speaking them will be a bad move but then, as I am contrary even with myself, I let them rip.

"IF YOU DON'T STOP RIGHT NOW…IF I HEAR ONE MORE WORD OUT OF YOU… I AM GETTING OUT OF

THIS CAR AND I AM WALKING BACK TO AUSTIN, TEXAS!"

Warren looks at me sideways. His lip curls. Possibly he is trying to stifle a giggle. Maybe it is a nervous giggle. Maybe it is a mocking giggle. Maybe there is no giggle at all lurking beneath the sound that slips out of his curled lip, a *pffft-ish,* gruntlike utterance. Technically this sound is not a word, and I have only said I will walk away if he says, "another word." But to ignore the sound would be to let him win. Win what, I have no fucking idea. All I know is I am pissed off and I now have two choices, both shitty. Shitty Choice A: Get out of the car and walk back to Austin, Texas, right now or Shitty Choice B: Stay in the car and lose.

I am a sore loser. You could already guess that, right? So I don't really have a choice at all. "FUCK YOU!" I yell, fumble with the front door handle, jump out, slam door, fumble with the backdoor handle, yank out my five-hundred-pound backpack, stumble away from car.

Ha! Now the ball is in Warren's court, as I leave him with two equal and opposite shitty choices! Shitty Choice A: Drive away from me, either just a little bit to pretend to abandon me or a lot to actually abandon me or Shitty Choice B: Follow me, giving me more fodder for my Angry Adolescent outburst.

As I hump it, my backpack too full with computer and books and knitting projects, pulling down on me like I'm a weary soldier marching off to the Western Front, I have a few unpleasant thoughts. For one, I still really need to pee. But to pee by the side of the road will mean giving in. Walking to a gas station— and who knows how far away one might be— will take far longer than if I'd stayed in the car. Also, I have precisely zero dollars on me, and zero in the account attached to my debit card, which I do have with me, so even if I am to walk back to Austin, this will necessarily involve calling someone to infuse my checking account with a big boost (and in the process exposing my idiocy to an outside witness).

Plus, *really*? Walking back to Austin? Even I can't whip myself into such a state of adolescence as to think I might be able to accomplish this. I mean, I'm a really, *really* good walker. But I can't cancel all the work I have scheduled back at home over the next few weeks. And though my iPhone is suffering from a low battery as well as ongoing bouts of out-of-range non-connectivity, I don't need a GPS to know I am a long fucking way from home. *A long, long fucking way.* (Later research confirms this via GoogleMaps Walking Directions, which suggest two possible foot routes—2,036 miles or 2,062 miles— each taking 27 days and change, both including a ferry and crossing into Canada, and neither including stopping to sleep, eat, or goddammit, PEE.)

So, okay, I know pretty much right off the bat, before I even slam the car door, that I am not walking back to Austin. Warren knows it, too. He opts to split the difference between his shitty options, alternately letting me get far enough ahead of him so as to be unable to see the Kia— giving the impression I'm on my own, out here in the woods ripe for the picking for rogue moose and psycho killer lumberjacks and methed out truckdrivers who, if they don't mow me down with their tree-laden tractor trailers, might just like to stop me for a quick rape before they head on their way— and then inching up, parallel to me, driving at 3 mph, sometimes calling out the window.

"Get in the car," he says.

He doesn't plead. He should plead. I ignore him.

"Just get in the car. Come on. Will you get in the car?"

Do I stop to yell at him? Probably. Who knows? My head is in that place where... oh *wait*, no it *isn't*. Sweet Irony! Marching along in a furious rage at a swift clip in the fresh crisp air has had an unwanted effect! Fuck you, fresh air! Fuck you, beautiful Fall colors! Fuck you, refreshing lack of humidity! I am feeling better. Decidedly better. Granted, my bladder is about forty seconds away from exploding, but damn, *I FEEL GOOD!*

Next thought: *Mustn't let Warren know I am feeling better. Mustn't let down my Fury Façade.*

But really, how long can this go on? GOT. TO. PEE.

The next time Warren creeps Shitty Shitty Putt Putt into view, he pulls up a little ahead of me. I give up. I get in the car. We are quiet. The fucking hotel, it turns out, is less than a mile away. Fifteen more minutes and I could've gotten there myself.

Chapter Sixteen

Back at the inn, I stake out a place in the lobby to sit and disappear into the internet for a while. We've already checked out of the room, so Warren heads off for somewhere else, I don't know where, his destination beside the point for either of us. We both need to cool off.

I answer a few emails, eavesdrop on a racist foursome of elder tourists, and stew in my juices. Some days I think self-analysis is an excellent tool, the thing I most need to grow, mature, calm down, be happy. This is not necessarily one of those days. Because I feel stuck in the analysis loop. Warren says, of such moments, when we are breaking down one event or another, "Let's analyze it til it sucks!"

Well, it already sucks. We've done it again, argued to the point of my Let's-Break-Up default setting, the one I know is rooted in wanting to never, ever be (or at least to never admit I am) dependent on another. I CAN TAKE CARE OF MYSELF! *I DON'T NEED ANYBODY!*

I don't want to be in this place. But analysis only gets me so far. Because it's one thing to recognize your feelings to see where you've gone wrong. But it's something else entirely to resolve to do anything about it. And something else far, far beyond that to take the steps necessary to execute the resolution.

I know this: I want an apology. I also know this: I myself do not wish to apologize. And I know that, much as I hate to admit it, an apology from me could go a long way toward salvaging the day. *Get back, Jojo, back to where you once belonged.* Or, better put, *get forward.* Move to a better place. *Get past this quickly as you can.*

Some tiny part of my brain, the part that is being entirely shouted down by the other part that wants me to keep fighting, knows that this current black mood is going to give way, sooner or later, to rational thought. But I can't just snap my fingers and get there. I am thinking it would be far easier to go home, break up, and live out my days Miss-Havisham-style, just me and the dogs and no involvement with any other people ever, order in all food and supplies from the internet, this being the only way to guarantee a life for myself that feels safe and in control.

I wallow in these obsessive thoughts, the only break coming from the racist retirees and another guy who is yelling into his cell phone. Maybe these annoyances are a strange blessing, as I can redirect some of my irritation at these idiot strangers.

Eventually Warren returns to retrieve me, suggests we go for a bite. As usual, he is ready to put the past in the past. As usual, I am prepared to re-engage. I explain to him that when I feel the way I feel now, I have no interest in eating. He doesn't need me to tell him this, he's heard it all before. He also knows that eating might not solve things entirely, but that considering my blood sugar is probably quite low, food won't hurt.

We wander over to the Red Potato, apparently one of the only food joints in town. The fare here is at best mediocre, hardly the sort of exquisite culinary delight to lift a funk. Still, the bland pasta helps some, carbs ever so slightly elevating my slumped spirits. By meal's end, I am ready to talk reasonably to Warren again.

On this, the penultimate night of our trip, we concur that we will head toward Portland, where we plan to spend our final day meeting up with Lisa, who runs the knitting retreats that first brought me to Maine. One last stop in Mooseville, though—Moose Lane. This bowling alley seems to serve as a town hub, featuring multiple bowling lanes, an arcade, a bar, a billiards room, a party room, and 22 huge TV screens mounted like modern day moose heads on the wall.

I'm just here for a t-shirt. There is a case full of them. "Want one of those?" I ask Warren, pointing to one that reads: Moose Knuckles.

Moose Knuckles, for those of you unlearned on the subject, is a slang term referring to the effect of too tight pants on a dude, when the scrotal sack becomes unfortunately outlined, clearly divided in a visible left-nut/right-nut configuration. Moose Knuckles are also known as the masculine version of Camel Toe, which as you can probably guess from context clues, is when chicks wear too-tight pants that overly and unfortunately accentuate their vulvic valley.

While I spend a decent amount of time in any given year suggesting that Warren tone down his adolescent humor and lay off randy jokes in mixed company, I have no qualms about playing the hypocrite and recommending this crass t-shirt. I rationalize my right to do this because the shirt recalls an incident I know he finds especially hilarious, a time years ago when he tried to explain the Moose Knuckle concept his father, an immigrant still learning some American idioms.

Warren says no the first time I ask if he wants a t-shirt. Without thinking, I ask again a few minutes later. And then I ask a third time. I don't even realize that I am setting myself up for him to point out that I am now doing exactly what he was doing when he repeatedly queried me about where I might like to stop and pee. When he does bring this up, there is no hostility, just amused irony and perhaps a little scorekeeping, a jovially faux-smug moment: *See, I don't get mad when you do it to me!*

Instead of getting defensive, my primary reaction in such instances, I fall back on my secondary response setting—apology. "Alright, alright, I *get* it. I'm sorry. Sorry, *okay*?"

Thankfully, we drift away from the topic before digging in too deep, distracted as we pull away from Moose Lane and set off to try to spot another moose or two before our journey south.

No luck. And now we are again driving in the dark, Warren at the wheel, and the rain is falling, and the speed limit signs seem to drop lower and lower as we crawl through the night. Playing with the radio station, I find some Classic Rock. Clapton comes on and, oh Age of Google, I can't help myself. I fish out my iPhone in this land of nature and transport myself back in time, to the sixties, hopping from one wiki page to another as I read aloud, for our trivia edification, random facts about Eric, and George Harrison, and the woman they fought over, and sundry other bits of pop flotsam and jetsam that mean nothing to us now and will mean even less five minutes hence as we forget, almost instantaneously, the information I am spouting.

But the distraction is nice, moves us away from dissecting our own relationship. The day has faded, and we are ready to sleep. As we debate when to stop and, more importantly where to stop, somehow we transition from mild outrage at Eric Clapton's shitty treatment of Patty Boyd to a debate over sleeping accommodations.

In Lewiston, a couple of hours south of Mooseville, and less than an hour from Portland, Warren pulls into a Motel 6. I don't hesitate, immediately informing him that I am not staying at a Motel 6. Why? Why am I putting down this chain motel that served me many times in the past, a place that allows dogs— which, even though the dogs aren't even with us, I still appreciate the policy— a place that in all likelihood will be at least on par with the motor lodge where we stayed the night before, and cost us less than half as much?

Probably my protest is rooted in some nascent principle I am formulating on the fly, a not yet fully gestated notion that I am worth more than this, that Warren should want us to stay someplace nice because *this is our vacation!* Warren is surely countering my thoughts with his own, reminding himself of the benefits of frugality, and feeling self-satisfied knowing that he is about to deliver us to a place that, by his estimation, ranks five stars, given that there is indoor plumbing.

Do I start yelling again? I can't remember, which more than likely means that yes, I start yelling again. Oh I am so pissed off. And I'm pissed off not just because he is going to win this round but because, yet again, I am reminded that he is the one laying out cash upfront for this trip, and even if I am going to reimburse him, I remain somewhat at his mercy.

Can this First World Problem get worse? You bet it can. Warren disappears into the office to secure a room, comes back, and says to me that he didn't pay the extra three dollars for wifi since he figured I wouldn't need it.

He figured WHAT? When has Warren ever known me to not need the internet. I NEED THE FUCKING INTERNET! Three lousy dollars? Three motherfucking stupid dollars? *No, really?*

Thus commences Explosion Number Two of the day. Can he not let go FOR ONE SINGLE DAY this goddamned frugality bullshit? Does he NOT KNOW that other men buy their women $5000 engagement rings? Am I not worth THREE LOUSY DOLLARS? What in the hell, what in the fuck, what in the WORLD is he thinking? DOES HE LIVE JUST TO TORTURE ME? Does he want me to start invoicing him for all the cheese and bread and mayonnaise he eats at my house? For the hot water he uses? Does he want me to send him a tally of the value of every free concert and play ticket I have ever acquired for him in my capacity as a writer? THREE DOLLARS! THREE MEASLY DOLLARS!

Holy shit. I am on fucking fire.

In the room, as we did the night before, we take separate beds, but this time it is not about a better night's sleep. This time it is about my rage. I rant for a while longer. I use my phone to look up reviews of this illustrious Taj Mahal of budget accommodations to which my partner has committed us and I discover that even the reviews are poorly written, with one barely literate commentator giving the joint a single star, complaining that there's not even a "chester drawers" here.

I burrow under the shitty, slick poly-cover, hide my head beneath this crappy pillow that god knows who slept on the night before. I send rage beams at Warren in hopes he will notice I am ignoring him. I try hard not to peek out and look at the TV show he's watching about Anna Wintour, the volume on way too loud. I fall into an enraged sleep. I wake up ready to swing some more. The "coffee," served free in the lobby along with the non-dairy "creamer," makes yesterday's liquid shit motor lodge coffee seem like espresso flown in piping hot from Italy.

But wait, am I not the reader of Buddhist tome upon Buddhist tome? Have I not just recently finished the slim volume by the doctor turned Buddhist nun? Do I not read these things in the hopes of learning how to let go? What is my problem? *Why can't I let go?* I know we have but one day left before us on this trip. I even know what's in store, a plan I've harbored for more than a year to take Warren around the islands that dot Casco Bay, off the coast of Portland. Somewhere inside of me, despite my anger, I think I know I love this man.

I know I do.

But fuck, I want to WIN. I want to just be right. I want always to be right. I want Warren to appreciate every fucking moment with me, every effort I make, every breath I take. And yes, fuck you, I know that in this rage I'm hardly providing him fuel for the love fire.

This is the place I hate most to be in my mind. I will never be a Buddhist. I will never escape my South Jersey roots, my raised-by-a-rage-a-holic legacy, my desire to always be right, a desire that I don't really want to admit to anyone (least of all myself) is rooted in fear. We are all scared little children so much of the time. Little child. Little child. Is this my problem? Is my rage at a $40 motel room somehow hinged on being told by my father my entire life that I am worthless? Or am I over-thinking this, wielding my English degree to look for symbolism where there is none?

Salvation comes in the form of a brief text exchange as we drive in bitter silence toward Portland. Remember *Who Wants to Be a Millionaire?* In particular, remember the whole lifeline thing? I get out my phone and send a text to Garreth, my Number One Secret Weapon against total relationship meltdown. Garreth came into my life via Warren, and we have had a running joke for four years now about how I stole Garreth away, made him mine.

Garreth has many pleasing qualities— an English accent that means he can be discussing overflowing litter boxes and it will sound lovely, ginger hair (my favorite), and that inimitable, dryer-than-toast and swifter-than-greased-lightning British wit. Over the course of our friendship, we have had countless relationship chats in which we have reminded each other, during respective rough patches, strategies to keep the center holding and things we most love about our partners who, as it happens, have a deep friendship of their own.

Not one to take sides, Garreth, an excellent listener, is perpetually able to find and gently dish up the broader view to counter my own myopia when I complain to him about Warren. Invariably, his counsel leaves me admitting my own role in relationship storms, laughing at myself, and ultimately backing down to a safer emotional plateau.

On this morning, I send a short text:

Well we knew it was bound to happen…I am seriously furious and spiraling into the rage hole. Any wise bon mot for me? This Buddhist shit isn't working.

His reply is swift, brief, and sound:

Breathe? Acknowledge that your mammalian brain has stopped working, and your communication and nurturing has been turned off. It's all reptile brain right now. Fight. Flight. So, don't try to talk. Just eat and stay warm.

I readily admit that if Warren issued the same advice, I would feel inclined to tear off his head while informing him that he is not the boss of me. But such is the beauty of outside counsel. I am not competing or arguing with or contemplating dumping Garreth on this seething drive. Those feelings are reserved for this man beside me, the one I allegedly love more than any other.

My reptilian brain! Unfamiliar with this term before, now I latch onto it. It's funny. It's fitting. It makes sense. I resume breathing as instructed. I choose to drop my angry silence and speak, and instead of telling Warren a list of things that are wrong with him, wrong with us, I tell him that we will be breakfasting at the Standard Bakery in downtown Portland. I say this in a tone that is neutral bordering on nice. To his credit, he doesn't contest me or question my choice as I consult the GPS and dictate directions that will usher us to this haven of confections.

The Standard is one of those bakeries that, if I lived near it, I would die of obesity or diabetes or both. There is not a bad choice in the case. The place first came on my radar on my virgin journey to Maine, when Patty, who co-hosts the knitting retreat, picked up a bunch of us at the Portland Jetport, loaded us into a big white van, and handed out crisp white bags with savory and sweet treats from the shop, including lobster-shaped sugar cookies. Now an annual pilgrimage for baked goods here is a must, and once inside I order up coffee— real coffee, true coffee, nothing like the shit-for-coffee "coffee" of the past two days— *pain au chocolat*, cookies, chocolate biscotti, some warm and doughy pretzely things, and, for our dinner later that night with Lisa and Patty, some obscenely delicious bread.

I eat. I drink coffee. I get warm even though we have opted to eat outside in the chilly air. Fat silver pigeons, not a trace of fear or shyness in their pudgy asses, boldly step up to swipe at our crumbs. The tears I shed on the drive here have dried. I give voice to a desire that we try to salvage the day. Warren says he's game, and wisely doesn't add that he's been game for this since I stormed back into the car up in Mooseville.

I think again about Warren's ability to shift gears seamlessly, to go from yelling one minute to being ready for fun the next. This is such a maddening trait in my eyes. Does it mean that when he is arguing with me that he's just kidding? Is it all about baiting me for the sake of some sick fun? No, that's not it. Because I can tell when he's mad, he truly is mad. But our central processing units are so wildly different, my own refusing to believe you can just snap one second then giggle the next. Does not compute.

And yet I know, I really do know, that if I am going to continue my life with this man (which I am going to, which I very much want to) then at some point I am going to have to resume liking him. I consider the evening moment in the Monhegan House, just days before, when he rubbed my feet and back and put music in my ears and I felt the refrain of early, giddy love. Didn't I tell myself to memorize that? Didn't I tell myself to call on it the next time we argued?

On the other hand, for as infuriating as it can be to have Warren cast off his anger like a dog shaking off a bath, I must admit this goes a long way toward swifter resolution. If we both held onto the ugly, then we'd stay stuck for a long time, definitely stay stuck this entire day, and miss out on the opportunities before us. I try to shove my residual resentment aside.

The storm clouds, literal and figurative, dissipate as we board the ferry for our ride around the bay. Billowy white tufts hover in a deep blue sky. Warren puts on a hat, a true sign that it's cold. Mostly we hunker down below, inside, away from the toothy wind. I knit away on my tricky orange honeycomb pattern scarf, and let myself be lulled by the water carrying us, and cheered by the treats I tug from their paper bag. Calming down. I am calming down.

An hour or so later, our cruise concludes, and we are back at the dock, best friends again. Now I give Warren a tour of downtown and remember the year before when I walked this route alone, silent, people-watching, the whole day to myself. Here we are now at Cousin Art's, the shop dedicated solely to cookbooks, where I foolishly try to engage one of the owners by telling him how much I loved Allegra Goodman's novel, *The Cookbook Collector*, which prompts in him a sigh of exasperation and a brief lecture on how wrong she got her details. I don't mind the speech so much, amused and pleased to know that, at least for now, there is still room in the world for tiny, independent stores owned by specialist curmudgeons with no patience for generalists like me.

Then off to Longfellow Books, where, inspired by the events of Trap Day on Monhegan Island, I ask for a good book about lobstering. The helpful clerk hands me a copy of *Tough Island* by Crash Barry, not a rich tome on the nitty-gritty of trapping, but more of a Hunter S. Thompson tale of the wasted days and wasted nights of a young man working for a grouchy ass cap'n.

A quick stop in KnitWits, the local yarn shop (Warren waits in the car). A failed attempt to get into the historic graveyard, unfortunately closed.

At each stop, we salvage the day a little more. We share chowder and root beer at a tourist stop. My tentative laughter turns to something more solid. We are going to be okay unless...

And here my mind reaches the last stage of the Big Argument Cycle. Not content to be content that things have settled down, now I allow suspicion to creep in. What if this playfulness Warren is exhibiting is some sort of fake Stockholm Syndrome? What if, just beneath the surface, his anger lurks like a bloodthirsty shark? What if he has decided that, in the interest of getting back to Austin without further incident, he is going to be all nicey-nicey and then, once we are back in our respective homes, he is going to text me a message along the lines of: *That's it! Finished! I'm tired of your bullshit!*

Why must my mind pull this on me? Why cannot I just accept and believe that this smoothing over between us is genuine?

"Look," I tell Warren, as we drive to Lisa's for dinner. "Not that I care…" (I open with this false sentiment as a sort of verbal talisman) "…but if you're just faking nice and you're planning to dump me when we get back, do me a favor and just get it over with now. Because I don't want to be nice to you on the plane if you're just going to be mean to me back in Austin."

Allow me to translate for me, here. What I think I am trying to say is something like this, "I am afraid of what went down yesterday and last night and this morning. I really, really hate this arguing shit. And even though we are getting better at recognizing the fights as they happen, and the patterns that cause them, and how to negotiate more swiftly back to terra firma, well even though all that… I am still afraid that you are going to leave me and I don't want you to leave me even though sometimes I think I want you to leave me because I love you even though sometimes it feels like I hate you and on top of all that I really never, ever want to admit that, god forbid, I need anyone for anything. DO YOU UNDERSTAND THAT?"

Warren reaches over to pat my knee. It is entirely possible that far more annoying and infuriating to him than the actual fighting and wall-of-silence aftermath is the neurotic fallout he has to endure when my brain short circuits as I try to over-process. Right now, he wants me to be quiet. Not *Shut Up* quiet. Just *Shhh, shhh, there, there it's going to be okay* quiet. I try to honor this, and to believe him when he tells me he's not playing nice just to trick me into submission. My kingdom for some ongoing peace, some way to really, truly finally believe that here is someone who is willing to stick around, the way no one else has done before.

Arriving at Lisa's house serves as the perfect tonic. Though we've only known each other a few years, and though we only see each other once a year, from the start we formed a solid friendship. Around her I am as comfortable being myself as I am with my closest friends back home.

We settle into the kitchen and I have a cup of coffee, which, given the late afternoon hour, is about as smart for me as a 7 am shot of whisky would be. Then Lisa breaks out the fancy chocolates. The conversation is fast and easy and silly and a little gossipy. Warren partakes as if he's known Lisa forever— this is why Lisa is so good at hosting retreats, her very nature inspires an instant letting down of guard.

She cooks while we chat and then the door knocks and in comes Patty. Patty holds a firm spot on my Top Five Most Grounded People I've Ever Met list. Unflappable, she is a genius at leading hikes all over Monhegan Island, of coaxing along even the most reluctant non-hiker, making the trails seem doable to the most vocal naysayers. We all sit down to a big bowl of pasta, and too many pieces of the hearty bread Warren and I brought from the Standard Bakery.

An hour passes, two. The pasta is making me sleepy, the conversation is making me laugh. These moments are the final joyful notes of our journey. My hyper vigilance has quieted, a rare thing, and instead of my monkey mind racing around for things to worry about— the arguments, the Faux Stockholm Syndrome theory and all the rest of it— I am genuinely in this moment, with my friends, with my partner.

Later on, Lisa will show us to our bed— her pullout sofa in the living room. Warren, miraculously, won't complain about it at all. In fact, he'll claim in the morning it is the best sofa bed he's ever encountered. For my part, I'll sleep like a dog that got into the Benadryl, right on through the night, this despite my taboo evening caffeine.

CHAPTER SEVENTEEN

Probably it says something about me that one of my favorite parts of traveling is heading to the airport to go back home, getting on the plane, catching the connecting flight, listening with the sort of ecstasy that should be reserved for proclamations that a war is over as the flight attendant announces, "Ladies and gentlemen, we are beginning our descent into Austin."

Part of my joy comes from the simple fact that I am in love with the city I call home. The jingoism— for Texas in general and Austin in particular— that I first witnessed without comprehension when I moved to the Lone Star State, long ago seized me, too. Maybe there's something in the water. But there is another component to the contentedness I feel, hinging on the feeling I've had more than once as I stood in a crushing crowd at a concert I initially could not wait to attend— *I can't wait for this to be over so I can go home and talk about it.*

What is this desire to be done with something in part so we can move on to the place where we get to describe it to others? Certainly not anything that has to do with being in the moment. But the storytelling, beyond being fun, is also an exercise in reflection that, hopefully, leads me to better myself. Do I love that I marched away from Warren in Mooseville? I do not. Does the story make people laugh? Uproariously. Does this make me angry? Actually, it makes me squirmy until I stop being squirmy. And then I laugh, too. And then, the next time I am feeling an urge to go stomping off, an echo of all this— the actual event, the event retold, the contemplation of the event— hopefully inspires me to make a different, less angry choice.

Despite my eagerness to get home, there is no rush to leave Lisa's house. I have finally gotten the hang of scheduling later flights whenever possible. I used to reason that flying out at the crack of dawn meant gaining time upon arrival, having the better part of the day on the ground. But after about two decades of predawn rushes, I finally came to understand how exhausting flying can be, more so when you wake at 4 am to catch a flight.

Now we take our time. There is more coffee, more laughter. We load our suitcases and Lisa takes us to the airport, an easy fifteen-minute drive from her house.

On the way we pass a Dunkin' Donuts, more ubiquitous in this part of the country than even McDonald's. We don't stop, but I still take some odd comfort in observing the tacky pink and orange sign. Dunkin' Donuts shops are an odd symbol of my Northeast upbringing. These little New England houses we're passing are another reminder, too. I come from small and crowded, harsh accents and attitudes, blue collars and processed food.

What trips me up too often, I realize, are the aspirations that sent me fleeing from this part of the world. No, no, I don't mean I regret the migration southwest, or the life I created that is in many ways the polar opposite of my eight siblings, most of whom stuck to the coast, to the stubborn ideals of our parents. But I have often judged them harshly from afar, wondered at their lack of enlightenment as I devoured my *New York Times*, immersed myself in NPR, squeezed my ass into yoga pants long before doing so became an annoying trend.

It's taken three decades of being gone to see that in running away from what seemed to me to be their unnecessary clutching of evil in the form of red meat, conservative politics, religion, and doughnuts, I have often over-clutched myself, grabbing onto the things I judged were "right," partly to cancel them out and partly because I really believed I could be better, smarter, and healthier than the people and place from which I came.

I still believe there is power and health in open-mindedness, green smoothies, liberal social policies, meditation and pigeon pose. But this Dunkin' Donuts makes me want to pull over, order a dozen (plus a box of holes), devour them all, give up yoga, and maybe, for good measure, get a bucket of KFC for dinner. Getting away from the home I've made in Austin, hip green bubble world that it can be, shakes me up like this, provides me with signs in unexpected places— like fast food fat factories— that live and let live is such a better, easier way to navigate this planet than finger-pointing and judging. Plus, I just sort of want a fucking jelly doughnut.

Warren takes a picture of me in the Portland Jetport, and it is a study in contrasts. This is one of those quaint airports dotted with big, bright white wooden rocking chairs and here I am, sitting in one, not knitting— which would be fitting— but fully immersed in my computer. Yes, I managed to put the damn thing down for long stretches over the past week. But my iPhone was never far from reach, not even the night we drove through the dark rain and I failed to resist an urge to investigate the former sex life of Eric Clapton. Will I ever break this habit?

Probably I will not.

Not only are Warren and I on the same plane home, we even manage to score seats together. Using my iPhone— my love, my bane!— I capture an image that might be more telling than any others taken on our trip. We both have our seatback screens tuned to a game of electronic Battleship, and the hilarious thing is this: because our screens are side-by-side, embedded into their frames, we cannot pull them down onto our laps. We cannot hide our moves from one another. There is no way not to see what the other one is up to, which robs us both of the ability to strategize.

And so, I realize, this is a silly but incredibly accurate metaphor for who we have become in our years together. There is no battle left in which we might genuinely outwit or outfight one another. We have learned each other inside and out, memorized the screens of one other's heart and mind. Which does not mean we will ever completely shelve the game. Sometimes, we are going to still whip out the boards, challenge each other, escalate. Sometimes I am going to get out of the car, slam the door, and holler. Sometimes, Warren is going to do the same.

I don't make these observations with resignation. I don't make them with exasperation. I make them with a knowing that edges toward something like the calm I am forever seeking. Things, I have finally learned, settle down if you give them time to settle down. I make this statement in a settled moment. I understand that when the next wave rage crashes in, I will forget the thought as if it never occurred to me in the first place.

Something I learned in therapy, back when I was naïve enough to believe the process could teach me how to stop fighting altogether, to just stay in the happy place, was a notion my therapist handed me regarding what she called "lag time." The key, she said, is not to end the arguing once and for all. In fact, she insisted this was impossible. Instead, the goal is to shorten the lag time, to get from I HATE YOU back to I LOVE YOU in shorter and shorter increments of time.

Does that sound simple to you? It sounded profound to me. I am such a black and white thinker. I had been in so many relationships that looked like this: fight, fight, fight, fuck, fight, fuck, fight, fight, fight, break up. I thought the opposite of this model, the thing to strive for, would be love all the time. Love, love, love.

During that Buddhist retreat, the one where I nearly punched out the lights of that condescending asshole, the one where the eighty-year-old nun laughed at my irritation, I also had the privilege of being in the same room as Thich Nhat Hanh. He gave a talk in which he explained to us that when we use the North Star for guidance, we don't expect to actually reach the North Star, we just use it to head in the right direction. Combining this graspable metaphor with the whole shortened-lag-time theory, I began, slowly to understand. Warren and I might never stop arguing, but perhaps we could learn to argue differently.

 He did not use the moment of landing to say, "Haha! I lied! I am breaking up with you, you bitch!" Though each of us, since that trip, has occasionally trotted out what once, and for a long time, was the old default setting: "Oh yeah! Well fuck you! I am LEAVING!"

 Nowadays when we argue, we are like tired old boxers too weary to land genuine punches anymore. We vaguely go through the motions, but it is as if we are watching ourselves in an out-of-body manner. I know what Warren is going to say. And for that matter, I know what I'm going to say. He knows what I'm going to say, too, and what he is going to say.

 We have, in this sense, become caricatures of who we were before. Warren usually picks up on the humor of this before I do. Then he laughs. Then I, still stuck a little in my old patterns, will decry his laughter and demand he be more serious. Then, probably, I will storm out of the room to sulk. But unlike times past, I won't last very long in my efforts. I want to say this is rooted in something profound, like the realization that our time on this planet is limited. Mostly though, I think it's just too exhausting to maintain the pace, too exhausting, too futile. Make love, not war. Score one for the hippies.

 So this is settling. You hear people say sometimes, regarding their mates, "I don't want to settle." I suppose they mean to say they don't want to settle for less than they think they deserve.

Maybe they should take the time to specify this. Because to me, *to settle* has revealed itself to be quite a desirable act, something that eluded me for much of my life. Living in a constant state of anxiety for as far back as I can remember mis-taught me to seek out and recreate unsettling circumstances so that I might remain in a familiar state.

Settling? I didn't even understand such a thing possible, until, one day, I did. In an odd way, the arguments guided me here, the anger my accidental North Star. Because only when I followed the anger, and when Warren went there with me, could I fully understand the utter blissfulness of the absence of anger. This has been the greatest trip of all, a rare instance where perhaps destination fully trumps journey. Accidental angle of repose.

And so, do they live happily ever after? Is this the sort of bliss to strike envy and resentment in the hearts of all the brokenhearted and hopelessly single?

Hell no. Because, it's only a matter of time before one of us gets the other going, not on purpose, but just because we will. Warren will ask me a question he feels is posed in innocence or jest, and I will interpret the query as him trying to control or mock or bait me. Or I will stop the car to offer unsolicited, unwanted "advice," which he will hear as a lecture. One of us will yell. The other will yell back. And then…

Well hopefully we'll get the lag time down to mere seconds. It used to take weeks. And then it took days. Sometimes nowadays, we can get from *I hate you* to *I'm sorry* to *I forgive you* in under an hour. Sometimes we can't. But the more we practice, the better we get. The fear subsides, the *Fuck You I'm Leaving* disappears. In this moment we will be angry. But in another, soon enough, we will not.

Acknowledgements

My life is an embarrassment of riches, to understate the matter. With each ensuing book, the list of whom to thank grows exponentially. In order to save untold trees, this time around I am going to offer a blanket thanks to everyone who has helped me along the way— you know who you are and I really wish you could all meet each other at the same time but that would require a stadium. Thank you. Thank you, thank you, *thank you*. For being my friend, for giving me work, for endless kindnesses, for patiently waiting for me to get my shit together (well, as much as it's going to be gotten together). Thank you.

I do want to thank a few groups and individuals specifically. When I started my writing workshop a couple of years ago, I never imagined that it would morph into the ongoing, cohesive group it has become. What a safe haven for true feelings, a hatchery for ideas, and a funny love club we have become. I couldn't have written this book without the encouragement and inspiration that flies around that studio every week. Thank you all.

Thanks to the cast members of the Dick Monologues past and present. Another sanctuary, another healing group. Who could've guessed that a show intended to run one night would still be going, six years later? *I love youse guys.*

To my sage English counselors: Garreth and Simon, for being on the receiving end of some mighty long emails. Thanks for talking me in off the ledge so many times.

To my design gurus: Erin Mayes who has created the single most badass book cover of all time; Michael Coker for being the best, most patient, most creative webmaster in the known universe, not to mention a spectacular friend and guiding light for many years; and to Ori Sofer for shooting the front cover image while being bossed around by me and the back cover image without my knowledge and knowing it would PISS ME OFF but, hey, damn if it didn't work out in my favor. Thank you!

Also a very special shout out to Dr. Kate, Deva Haney, Sandy Rankin and Nancy Parker-Simons—all of y'all have had a major hand in convincing me and inspiring me to publish this one myself. Eternal gratitude for the encouragement.

To the far-flung folks who take time to cheer me on from a distance, in particular the St. Louis contingent, the D.C. contingent—I'm talking to you Hank Stuever. And thanks to my friends in Maine—Lisa for introducing me to the place, Holden and Sue for making me feel so at home, everyone on Monhegan Island for making that place so magic, and my DF contingent, who shall remain unnamed but I can't wait to see you again soon.

Thanks as ever to the inner-sanctum of first responders who are there in a moment's notice— Michael "Big Red" McCarthy, Ross, Emily Vaughan, Jill & Kenan, Kat, Chris, MJGJ, Em & Bug, Erin & Steve, Mike & Claudia, Ann Woodall, Katherine Martinez, Makoto, Sarah Barnes, David & Ken, and Chris McDougall.

Thanks to all of y'all who kicked in on KickStarter to make this happen—I felt a little weird asking but damn, I feel GREAT now! So excited to see this project through.

A very big thanks to my Anonymous Angel, who always prefers not to be named and who has continuously provided a ridiculous amount of support of every stripe over the years. THANK YOU.

And huge thanks to Paula & Jay for providing me with a writing garret in Galveston and to Heather & Martin Kohout who granted me a writing residency at Madroño Ranch. Being able to run away to the beach and the ranch was tremendously helpful in taking on the daunting tasks of editing and revising.

Of course I can't have an acknowledgements page without giving a big shout out to my Mom—Hi, Mom! And my son—Hi, Henry Mowgli! Thank you both. Mom, I'll be home to visit soon! Henry, please come home to visit soon!

Ori Sofer has been more than a good sport through the many years that we've loved and lost (our tempers) and loved some more. He once saved me from a wild donkey and many times has saved me when I've made a wild ass of myself. Monkey? Here it is in print: I promise, cross my heart, that I will never, *ever* marry you. (You're welcome.)

And finally, I want to thank my dear friend Isabel— our time together was entirely too short, but your impact was profound and is lasting. Thank you, Isabel, for giving me the gift of your healing. I am forever grateful.